Promoting Inclusion and
Diversity in Early Years Settings

# Promoting Inclusion and Diversity in Early Years Settings

A Professional Guide to Ethnicity, Religion, Culture and Language

## Chandrika Devarakonda

**Jessica Kingsley Publishers**
London and Philadelphia

First published in Great Britain in 2021 by Jessica Kingsley Publishers

An Hachette Company

3

Copyright © Chandrika Devarakonda 2021

Front cover image source: Shutterstock®. The cover image is for illustrative purposes only, and any person featuring is a model.

A CIP catalogue record for this title is available from the British Library and the Library of Congress

ISBN 978 1 78592 423 1
eISBN 978 1 78450 801 2

Printed and bound in Great Britain by CPI Group (UK) Ltd, Croydon CR0 4YY

Jessica Kingsley Publishers' policy is to use papers that are natural, renewable and recyclable products and made from wood grown in sustainable forests. The logging and manufacturing processes are expected to conform to the environmental regulations of the country of origin.

Jessica Kingsley Publishers
73 Collier Street
London N1 9BE, UK

www.jkp.com

# Contents

# Acknowledgements

I have been very lucky to have been around several people who have influenced me immensely and in a positive manner.

First and foremost, I would like to thank my father for inspiring me, by being a role model, instilling confidence and supporting me consistently and blessing me. Although I can feel your presence, I do miss your constant reassurance. My mother has motivated me to believe in myself and encouraged me to do my best. Thank you very much for instilling good moral values and the importance of staying positive. I'd also like to thank my father-in-law and mother-in-law, for their affection and kindness in all my endeavours.

I would like to thank my husband Prasad for helping me to focus, supporting me through the difficult times, persevering and being patient. Anuradha, my daughter, for being understanding and for influencing my ideas by discussing her experiences and understanding.

My mentors Mrs Varalakshmi and Mr Ramaswami (who have left us) for their support, and Prof. Jeyachandran for enabling me to believe in my abilities. My extended family and friends for constantly reminding me that their support is available.

I would like to thank Dr Marlies Kustatscher for her constructive comments; my students: Rachel Webster for her constructive feedback on the draft, Llinos for contributing to one of the chapters and also your comments, and Charlotte Brophy for your observations and also discussions we had inside and outside classrooms. Colleagues and students from the University of Chester and other universities around the world, who have influenced my ideas through thought-provoking discussions and responding to my requests for information.

Last, but definitely not least, thanks to Jessica Kingsley Publishers for the opportunity. A special mention to Jane Evans for being supportive and understanding through the journey of writing this book. In the last few years, I have lost some of the most important and influential people in my life, but your constant encouragement ensured I did not falter in my focus.

# Introduction

Migration and globalisation have resulted in increased diversity of the population in many developed countries (Nargis and Tikly, 2010). The increase in migration into Europe, which includes families with young children, is due to a range of factors, including economic migration, people seeking asylum and/ or those fleeing political unrest or war (refugees) (Nargis and Tikly, 2010). The rapid change in social, cultural and political context in the receiving countries like the United Kingdom and other European countries implies that early years and primary education settings are highly diverse and exceedingly culturally rich learning communities (Nargis and Tikly, 2010). For example, in England, net migration in 2018 showed an increase of 29 per cent over the previous 15 years (DfE, 2018). This led to an increase in the diversity of pupils, from the perspective of their ethnicity, socioeconomic status, religious backgrounds and English as an additional language in primary and secondary schools (Nargis and Tikly, 2010). This has resulted in an additional expectation on teachers to acknowledge and identify the diverse and unique needs of all children. Further, teachers will have to understand the need to relate to and appreciate the diverse backgrounds of the pupils in the classroom and provide opportunities to include them. But do teachers feel prepared to teach in diverse settings?

Diversity refers to children who are from different contexts and backgrounds and have different needs and abilities.

This includes ethnicity, gender, age, disabilities, race, religion, Gypsy, Roma and Traveller families and other categories. Paine (1990) proposed four categories of diversity perceived as layers:

- individual differences – relating to biological and psychological dimensions such as being tall, shy, etc.

- categorical differences – belonging to specific categories such as class, ethnicity and gender

- contextual differences – defined by social contexts and are socially constructed

- pedagogical view of difference – relating to how the differences found in individuals and groups have implications on their teaching and learning experiences.

UNESCO highlighted diversity in its definition of inclusion:

> as a process of addressing and responding to the diversity of needs of all learners through increasing participation in learning, cultures and communities, and reducing exclusion within and from education. It involves changes and modifications in content, approaches, structures and strategies, with a common vision which covers all children of the appropriate age range and a conviction that it is the responsibility of the regular system to educate all children. (2005, p.13)

Promoting inclusion and diversity means acknowledging and respecting differences. Diversity can be promoted through a set of conscious practices that involve:

- understanding that the needs of people belonging to specific groups are not homogenous

- mutual respect for people and experiences that are different

- recognising that individual and institutionalised

discrimination will result in privileges for some while others are disadvantaged

• building bridges, which can eliminate all forms of discrimination.

Examples of categories related to diversity in a community related to children and families:

| Gender | Race | Ethnicity | Culture |
|---|---|---|---|
| EAL | Socioeconomic status | Area of residence | Levels of education of parents |
| Looked after child | Foster care/ adopted | Ability/ disability | Migrant/ refugee/asylum seeker |
| Country of origin | Age | Religion | |

Sometimes, children are assigned a label and are considered disadvantaged or vulnerable as a result of stereotyping. The needs of children cannot be assumed based on their visible characteristics. For example, all 'White' children are not privileged and advantaged.

Diversity can be perceived to be in several layers. These layers can be visible or invisible due to overlap of categories or over-emphasis of certain categories.

Figure I.1 highlights layers showing the categories the child belongs to and the influence of these categories on the child. The child can be covered by several categories of labels and experience discrimination. The categories overlap, which can result in the child being identified with a specific label(s) rather than seen as a holistic child. Some categories seem to rise above others in different contexts, especially home and school/ early childhood settings. Some people might focus on certain categories and homogenise the needs of the child. Further categories can be added that are relevant to people and are considered important to identify themselves. Some categories will have greater relevance and significance for some groups of people (e.g. ability will be more obvious to teachers; gender will be significant to peers).

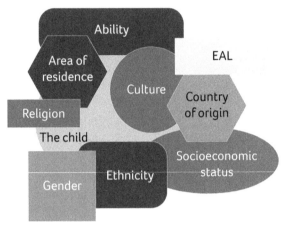

*Figure I.1: Categories of labels attached to children*

A child might be labelled as belonging to some of the above categories. Their perception relating to these categories might vary depending on the context of the setting. A child might relate to one or two categories that they identify with when comparing themselves to others. For example, Lauren, a three-year-old girl, might classify herself as a girl with curly hair. Other children might refer to Lauren as a kind and cheerful child. A parent might emphasise one or two other categories such as gender or ability, and that might be different to how a friend/peer or a practitioner/professional might highlight more visible categories relevant to learning and development. Once a child is labelled, stereotypes associated with that label can influence how the child is perceived.

## ● CASE STUDY

A three-year-old girl, Maaya, has Down syndrome. She lives in London and attends a private nursery. Her parents are from Malaysia and Italy.

Maaya might identify herself as a girl who loves dance and music.

Peers might identify Maaya as a three-year-old girl who has curly hair, is funny and is their friend.

Practitioners and professionals might see her as a disabled child with Down syndrome (maybe because of noticeable characteristics), who speaks English as an additional language (EAL). How they see her may also depend on the professional they are discussing her with, such as the speech therapist, educational psychologist, special educational needs co-ordinator (SENCO) or general practitioner (GP).

Her parents might relate to most of the attributes of the child such as gender, ethnicity, culture, religious affiliation and EAL ability.

Most of these attributes are visible. Some of these attributes can be more visible than others. How visible they are also depends on the individual's perspectives influenced by their knowledge and understanding, experiences and exposure to diversity.

It is important to see Maaya as a child with all of the above attributes – some of them are positive and others can be seen as weaknesses. Maaya's attributes are unique and may not be similar to other children with Down syndrome or who speak English as an additional language or have a particular religious affiliation.

Labels are useful to meet the needs of children, but if they are used inappropriately, the labels can be disabling (Hessels, 1997). Lauchlan and Boyle (2007) addressed the benefits of labelling from the perspective of special education. They listed arguments and counter-arguments as shown in Table I.1.

**Table I.1: Advantages and disadvantages of labelling**

| Advantages | Disadvantages |
|---|---|
| Diagnosis, or a label, will help to access treatment and specialist resources. | Despite the label, relevant intervention and support needed may be missing. |
| Labelling raises awareness and understanding of particular difficulties. | Labelling might harm the individual as a result of stigma. |
| Labels enable professionals to relate to the specific condition rather than generalising or stereotyping. | All professionals may not perceive a label in the same way. |
| Labels provide a solution to a problem and can be reassuring for children and families. | Labelling focuses on the child's weaknesses and so lowers expectations. |
| Labels allow individuals to develop an identity: a sense of belonging to a group. | Labels can lead to discrimination, bullying, exclusion and low self-esteem. |

One of the key challenges faced by teachers and schools has been dealing with the heterogeneous nature of diversity of children in the classrooms. Teachers might consider diversity a problem due to their limited knowledge and understanding as well as feeling unprepared to teach all children. Further, the early years workforce is predominantly White people, who might relate to diversity in a homogenous manner influenced by their narrow perceptions of diversity.

# WHEEL OF INCLUSION – STRENGTHS-BASED MODEL

Focus on strengths rather than weaknesses
Who drives (active involvement)
What accelerates
Brakes/breaks
Spokes:
  influences
  attitudes
  commitment
Knowledge and understanding
Training and skills

*Figure I.2: Wheel of inclusion*

Inclusion as a concept has been evolving in the last few decades and perceptions of it have changed. The wheel of inclusion helps to illustrate this concept. The wheel must be on the move constantly ensuring everyone in the community – i.e. children and their families, teachers, administrators, policy makers, researchers – is included. For the wheel of inclusion to move constantly and forward, it is important to ensure that everyone who is facilitating the wheel's movement must work around the inclusive philosophy.

The spokes holding the wheel together are the major influences. The spokes relate to the attitudes of people towards inclusion, commitment, knowledge and understanding relating to the needs of the child, resources available, as well as training and skills to teach children from a wide range of backgrounds.

Everybody has strengths and weaknesses. It is important to focus on strengths and build on them to overcome the weaknesses. But there is a tendency to highlight the weaknesses of an individual and overlook the strengths. For example, when looked at through the lens of the medical model of disability, a child diagnosed with a visual disability is likely to be presumed to be unable to do many things. The child may be assumed to struggle in their basic routine activities and need support. The strengths of the child might be overlooked. Although the child might not be able to see (which would restrict the child's ability to do several things in his or her daily routine, accessing resources), they may be able to be independent with the support of an adapted environment and appropriate resources. The same child may also have strengths related to other senses such as hearing or touch, as well as other abilities such as art, craft, poetry, etc. For example, the English poet Helen Keller, popular singer Stevie Wonder, famous painter Claude Monet and scientist Stephen Hawking were very successful in their fields despite their disability. This might have been in part due to the support and encouragement provided by their teachers and parents to develop to the best of their potential.

## Who drives the wheel of inclusion?

There is a wide range of people involved in the process of inclusion and who are responsible for driving inclusion forward. Some of them are directly involved at the grassroots level. Government, politicians and policy makers are engaged in developing policies and legislation influencing inclusion. Professionals based in support services, as well as school staff – head teachers, teachers and support staff – and parents are involved in implementing inclusion. The more hands on the wheel of inclusion at different levels, the faster and efficient it will be. It is important to ensure everyone is having a key role in moving the wheel of inclusion forward by including children, parents, practitioners/teachers and support professionals and administrators at all levels.

The key to successful inclusion is commitment, positive attitudes and good intentions from the people involved. If an individual or institution does not have the right attitude or commitment, it might result in merely tokenistic inclusion. The wheel of inclusion might slow down because of temporary loss of momentum or even long term due to breakdown or the brakes being applied on the process of inclusion.

## Visible and invisible diversity

It is important to be aware of both visible and invisible forms of diversity. Visible forms of diversity are easy to label, and therefore it is easy to develop prejudices and stereotypes about them. Invisible diversity describes some of the categories that may not be obvious and that might also mask the individual needs of the child. Invisible forms of diversity include attributes or characteristics such as cultural diversity, religious beliefs and educational levels that may not be explicit on initial exposure to the individual and may thus lead to stereotyping. The adults supporting the child must acknowledge and identify all the needs of the children considering the visible and invisible diversity rather than homogenising under the child's needs under the visible category. Bias and prejudice can be avoided by being open and engaging in dialogue to be able to relate to invisible diversity.

Hamilton (2013) conducted qualitative research in Welsh rural primary schools to identify the experiences of children and parents of Eastern European heritage and their teachers with limited exposure to cultural and linguistic diversity. Findings indicated that 'children become so integrated into UK schools that their *individual* learning needs, well-being and heritage are at risk of being overlooked' (p.205). Hamilton believes that the needs of these children were overlooked due to 'invisibility', and the reasons might include the following: limited information on children's prior learning, ability and attainment; children being camouflaged by shared language peers; insufficient guidance for more orally advanced learners; inadequately trained practitioners; teachers' perceptions of cultural homogeneity; and children's intra-group dependency.

Monolingual assessments, based on English-speaking British middle-class norms and educational expectations, have long been criticised for their failure to accurately reflect the academic potential of migrant children (Loewen, 2004; Sikan, 2007; Siraj-Blatchford and Clarke, 2000). These strategies will result in devaluing the strengths possessed by minority language pupils, leading to these children becoming demoralised and not engaging with their learning process.

An increase in migration in the last decade will have raised practitioners' and professionals' awareness about diversity and their ability to meet the needs of children from different backgrounds. This migration has also resulted in an increased number of children speaking languages other than English as their first language or mother tongue. Teachers expressed the need for training to enable them to support migrant children, identify specific learning differences, communicate with parents and use appropriate teaching strategies (Manzoni and Rolfe, 2019). The feasibility of recruiting staff who are able to speak in the wide range of languages spoken in a setting might be questioned. Further, identification of special educational needs (SEN) and medical conditions of children speaking English as an Additional Language (EAL) can be complicated, as teachers might struggle to differentiate between EAL and SEN. The inability of EAL children to respond to assessments mainly in English may also be diagnosed to be a learning difficulty. In addition, teachers' ability to provide adequate and relevant support can be compromised due to being misled by perceptions of cultural homogeneity.

Will it help to recruit teachers from diverse backgrounds to identify and meet the needs of all children? The Organisation for Economic Co-operation and Development (OECD) recently highlighted that it has been challenging to recruit teachers from minority backgrounds in several developed countries (OECD, 2017). Table I.2 shows challenges experienced at different levels from the perspective of teachers, schools and the government that may enable or, if lacking, become barriers in meeting the needs of children from diverse backgrounds. These challenges located at different levels of a country are interrelated and influence services provided in the community.

**Table I.2: Challenges faced by teachers, schools and government in meeting the needs of children and families from diverse backgrounds**

| Teachers | Schools | Government |
|---|---|---|
| Awareness of diverse children and families – backgrounds, contexts and experiences | Wide range of resources<br>• Awareness<br>• Access | Developing policies to reflect the changing contexts of the country |
| Confronting own perceptions of stereotypes and prejudices around diversity | Partnership with families and local communities | Adapt curriculum content to reflect diverse communities |
| Preparedness to teach children from diverse backgrounds | Prioritising training for teachers | Ensure appropriate teacher training is developed |
| Opportunities to share good practice | Ethos and philosophies influencing inclusion | Developing clear channels of communication at all levels |

## MODEL OF AWARENESS OF DIVERSITY

This model has been developed for identifying and raising awareness about diversity in teachers, practitioners and professionals working with children and their families from diverse contexts and backgrounds. Adapting the model of Johari Window, this model emphasises acknowledging the heterogeneous nature of diversity and identifying the differences in the individuals and being able to identify and confront one's own stereotypes and prejudices (see Figure I.3).

|  | Known by self | Unknown by self |
|---|---|---|
| Known by others | Open and free (stereotypes and prejudices) – what we do know is open and flexible to adapt to new information<br><br>Visible diversity – what is politically correct, attitudes to diverse population | Blind spot – you are prejudiced and do not necessarily believe you are prejudiced<br><br>Religious diversity, ethnic minorities, EAL, Gypsy, Roma and Traveller families<br><br>Perceived by others – especially the members of diverse communities |
| Unknown by others | Façade or mask (hidden) – you are prejudiced, but do not like to admit to your prejudices because they are not acceptable in society<br><br>Attitudes towards specific diverse groups – Gypsy, Roma and Traveller families, ethnic minority groups, specific religions | Unknown by self and others – you do not know that you hold some stereotypes because it is unconscious<br><br>Invisible diversity – ingrained by society, lack of awareness<br><br>Perceived by others – especially the members of diverse communities |

Adapted Johari Window model to develop an understanding of challenges to relate to the perspectives of diversity.

*Figure I.3: Model of awareness of diversity*
Adapted from Luft, J., Ingham, H. (1955) 'The Johari window, a graphic model of interpersonal awareness.' *Proceedings of the Western Training Laboratory in Group Development.* Los Angeles: University of California, Los Angeles.

This model can be used by individuals or organisations to identify gaps in knowledge and understanding. It can inform training, discussions and workshops in raising awareness of diversity among practitioners and teachers.

## THE NEED FOR THIS BOOK

Globalisation has resulted in an increase in migration of people to keep safe from volatile war zones and for better job opportunities in multinational companies. The increase in global migration and displacement of families has resulted in linguistic and cultural diversity of communities and classrooms. So, early childhood settings and schools are attended by children from diverse ethnic, cultural, religious, linguistic and socioeconomic backgrounds.

This requires the early childhood practitioners and teachers to be aware of and be able to meet a wide range of needs and to teach all children effectively. Therefore, they must be provided with opportunities to share knowledge and raise awareness of diversity. This helps to develop knowledge and understanding, to appreciate and respect similarities and differences across various racial, ethnic and religious groups in a diverse society (O'Connor & Zeichner, 2011; Suárez-Orozco, 2001).

This book explores a child from a holistic perspective. Diversity is unpacked from a wide range of perspectives such as race and ethnicity, culture, EAL, religion and intersectionality. References will be made to theoretical base, legislation and policies, good practice, challenges faced by practitioners, teachers and professionals working with children and their families, and some practical advice will be given to support them.

Key issues discussed include the rights of the child, challenges perceived around teaching diverse children, teaching children about diversity, recruiting staff from diverse backgrounds, involving parents and families from different backgrounds, and the importance of acknowledging, valuing and respecting parents and families of children from minority groups.

# 1

## Race and Ethnicity

This chapter will focus on:

- the relevance and the concept of race and ethnicity and how it is interpreted in different contexts – early years and primary years

- the theoretical base around children's awareness of race

- development of children's identity, attitudes and expectations towards stereotypes and prejudices towards minority groups

- perspectives of practitioners in including children from diverse backgrounds

- challenges faced by practitioners/teachers and parents

- sharing good practice that will guide and help with resolving problems and difficulties.

Migration has been taking place for centuries. Migration patterns differ across ethnic groups and religions. It is important to note that there are numerous reasons for this, such as historic or commonwealth ties; legislative changes; and personal, economic and cultural events. It is also related to international politics, events and conflicts (ONS, 2011a). Save the Children (2016) reports that millions of children flee from their home country, accompanied or unaccompanied by adults, for safety and protection from war, violence, poverty and/or disaster. Children make up a third of the global population, but they make up half of the world's refugees. A CNN report by McKirdy (2016) shows statistics reporting that 50 million refugee children worldwide were displaced, both with and without families. The last five years saw a 75 per cent increase, resulting in 8 million child refugees due to global conflicts. Ongoing war and conflicts in Syria and Afghanistan have resulted in child refugees. Several countries around the world have welcomed children and their families but are struggling to protect them from being discriminated against and excluded. In 2015, the UK accepted 750,000 children under 18 years old (Hodal, 2016).

## Reflection point

Is there a danger and a possibility of homogenising the needs of all children who have migrated as refugees? Would these children be stereotyped?

The 2011 Census enabled an individual to identify with an ethnic group and religious affiliation that is self-defined and emotionally meaningful to that individual. A UK resident who was born outside the UK has migrated to the UK at some point in the past. While some non-UK-born people will have migrated recently, others will have lived in the UK for many years and gained UK citizenship. This can lead to an identity conflict for the child from the perspective of their race and ethnicity. Teachers and practitioners face a dilemma about whether it is acceptable to ask people about their ethnicity and background but not their race (Vega, 2017). Poor knowledge and understanding about race and ethnicity may be the reason why teachers can feel that discussing issues around race with children is uncomfortable and rude (Priest et al., 2016).

## THE CONCEPTS OF RACE AND ETHNICITY

Race is a socially and politically constructed way of grouping people, which differs from country to country (Wardle and Cruz-Janzen, 2004). Ethnicity, on the other hand, is a shared cultural worldview and/or people with the same geographical origin. The concept of race is flawed (Hirschman, 2004) as this does not have a 'logical basis' 'as a social category' (p.408).

Race has been used loosely as it does not relate to categories based on national, religious, linguistic or cultural groups (UNESCO, 1950a). Hirschman (2004, p.389) states that: 'Racism is a structure of belief that the "other community" is inherently inferior and lacks the capacity to create a society comparable to one's own.' Cox, Tayles and Buckley (2006) feel that racism exists because of the 'flawed reasoning that the biological variation so visible in humans translates into differences in abilities or behaviour' (p.869).

Race and ethnicity are modern concepts. They have origins in the global expansion of European societies from the late 15th century onwards, but emerged in the modern form between the end of the 18th and the middle of the 19th centuries. 'This concept of difference became inextricably linked to a notion of hierarchy in which all differences both of history and future potential were seen as a product of biological variation' (UNESCO, 1950b, p.7). Anthropologists divided humanity into three categories of races – the Mongoloid, the Negroid and the Caucasian (UNESCO, 1950b). These categories are not static and are no longer in use as the concepts have become politically incorrect and unacceptable.

The terms race and ethnicity are controversial. People have been categorised to determine their place in a hierarchy that defines if they are privileged and empowered or not. Categorising people has resulted in conflict within and between groups due to prevailing stereotypes and prejudices related to different races.

However, the word 'race' is used with quotation marks by some authors as an acknowledgement that it is a controversial and contested term (Advance HE, 2019).

Ethnicity differs from race, nationality, religion and migrant status, sometimes in subtle ways, but may include facets of these other concepts (Bhopal, 2003). According to the House of Lords (HRCR, 1983), an ethnic group has the following features:

- a long-shared history of which the group is conscious as distinguishing it from other groups and the memory of which it keeps alive

- a cultural tradition of its own including family and social manners, often but not necessarily associated with religious observance

- a common, however distant, geographical origin

- a common language and literature.

Some of the key differences between race and ethnicity are listed in Table 1.1.

It is important to be aware of how race and ethnicity are referred to in different parts of the world. It seems to be inconsistent, as the European Union uses race and ethnicity synonymously. People may be labelled as belonging to a specific ethnic group, but the individual might identify as belonging to a different ethnic group. A wide range of categories has been added to the census, to enable people to identify themselves confidently. Bhopal warns that 'race should be used with caution for its history is one of misuse and injustice' (Bhopal, 2003, p.442).

**Table 1.1: Differences between race and ethnicity**

| Race | Ethnicity |
|---|---|
| Is categorised according to skin colour and physical characteristics – bone structure, eye colour | Individual's identification with a group |
| Determined by how you look (physical characteristics) | Cultural factors, nationality, regional, ancestry and language<br><br>Ethnicity relates to how people identify themselves and how they are seen by others |
| Fewer races | Thousands of ethnic groups |
| Hierarchical classifications of human beings | Self-defined |
| Emotive and contested term | Can evolve over time |
| Socially constructed | Differences in perceptions of ethnicity between self and others |
| Controversial | Some countries encourage people to define themselves – e.g. in the UK, the census allows people to choose options of ethnicities that closely define them |
| Not widely referred to by self or others | Used to identify readily |

Ethnicity of a person describes the group he or she belongs to as a result of a mix of cultural factors including language, diet, religion and ancestry. However, in English-speaking countries such as the United Kingdom, United States of America, New Zealand, Australia and Canada, despite the differences in their country of origin, religion and culture, people can be stereotyped and identified on the basis of their skin colour and being an

English speaker. There will be local and cultural influences that might differentiate their perspectives of identity.

In the UK, according to a briefing from CODE (Centre on Dynamics of Ethnicity at the University of Manchester), the term ethnic minority group is used to refer to minority populations who are not White and are of non-European origin (University of Manchester, 2013).

Some of the categories related to ethnicity are perceived in different ways in different countries. For example, the United Nations reported that 65 per cent of countries categorised their population by national or ethnic group (United Nations Statistics Division, 2003 cited in Morning, 2015). A wide range of terms were used to categorise people, such as 'race', 'ethnic origin', 'nationality', 'ancestry' and 'indigenous', 'tribal' or 'aboriginal' group. For example, the term Asian relates to people from different regions of Asia – East Asia, Southeast Asia or South Asia. In the UK, it refers to people with roots from South Asia, especially the Indian subcontinent – India, Pakistan, Bangladesh and Sri Lanka (Simpson, Jivraj and Warren, 2016). Hoeffel *et al.* (2012) quote the US Office of Management and Budgets (OMB) to define 'Asian' as referring 'to a person having origins in any of the original peoples of the Far East, Southeast Asia, or the Indian subcontinent, including, for example, Cambodia, China, India, Japan, Korea, Malaysia, Pakistan, the Philippine Islands, Thailand, and Vietnam' (p.2).

Historically, racial and ethnic groups have been considered homogenous by Western countries. There has been a tendency to classify people into broad racial or ethnic groups (e.g. Black African) and not take into account the cultural differences between those groups. The heterogeneous nature of individuals within specific groups may remain unnoticed. For example, a Black person from Uganda might have totally different cultural, linguistic and social context compared to another Black person from Nigeria. A White person from England might have different perspectives of identity compared to another White person from Hungary. Further, Simpson *et al.* (2016) suggest that the ethnicity of an individual is evolving, especially between people belonging to different generations.

Race and ethnicity are social constructs (Kaplan, 2011). Terms and concepts are evolving and developing constantly; which terminology is considered acceptable or politically correct changes and differs across time and place. For example, people with darker skin are referred to as Black in the UK and colored (American spelling) in the USA. This term 'colored' is not perceived as derogatory in the USA and aims to be inclusive of non-White people as well as people of mixed parentage and ancestry. So, it is important to use the terms and concepts with care and be aware of what is acceptable. It is interesting to note that in some countries the ethnic minority groups are sometimes categorised based on colour – Black African/Caribbean – and sometimes based on their national origin – Indian, Pakistani, Bangladeshi. According to Philips (2015), terminology such as Black and minority ethnic (BME) and Black, Asian and minority ethnic (BAME) used in the UK is 'outdated' and believes these terms to be 'divisive' and perhaps 'mask the disadvantage suffered by the minority groups'. He recommends adopting terms such as 'visible minorities' or 'people of colour' which are used in the USA. However, BME and BAME are used inconsistently in different contexts in the UK.

Advance HE (2019) provides some guidance on their website about using appropriate terminology around race and ethnicity. It is clear from their website that the guidance does not reflect the worries articulated by Philips (2015). In my view, the terms race and ethnicity are loosely used as they have been used interchangeably. Further, it depends on how individuals and society relate to these concepts (Bryce, 2020).

## IDENTITY – WHO AM I?

The UK is a society comprised of many cultures, values, attitudes and beliefs (Knowles, 2011); it is also the society that acknowledges that such diversity can engender discrimination. Hinman (2003) states that 'race, ethnicity and culture are central to one's identity', and 'identity is central to one's sense of self' (p.343).

'Who am I?' can be a complicated question to answer. How does a child or adult respond to this question? How does an adult identify themselves? Do they relate to their gender, race, ethnicity, religion, nationality or any other group they belong to? Does a migrant holding a passport of the domicile country by personal choice following naturalisation change their identity and give up their original identity?

Do we gain our identity based on where we live, country of birth, the country where our parents were born or their ancestry or heritage? What if both parents are from different countries, ethnic groups and races? If the family is originally from one country, but lives in a different country for several generations – what and how will the child's identity be? Will they develop dual or multiple identities? What will be the impact of this on the child's personality – confused or proud to be able to relate to both identities and be able to relate to their identities in different contexts?

### Reflection point

Are there any differences in the perceptions of identity – how you see yourself and how others see you? Is an individual's identity mainly determined by skin colour and physical features?

The term identity has different meanings. For example, a family from Wales living in England may prefer to identify themselves as Welsh rather than British irrespective of how long they have lived in England and even though Wales is part of the United Kingdom. Another child's family migrating from India for higher education or migrating for a job in health or the IT sector might have a dual identity of being Indian at home and British outside the home. When this person identifies as British, there is always a question – 'But where are you originally from?' This has been voiced by migrants across the continents, and this question is 'both loaded and personal' and is usually a 'question that people of colour, and anyone with an accent', is asked (Wong, 2019; also see Vega, 2017). Vega (2017) believes this question to be a form of microaggression and she adds her critical perspective that 'people like me are being too sensitive about harmless, everyday questions'. This might suggest curiosity as well as an interest in determining the background of the individual, especially if someone is not a White person. Would this help them to relate to the person or enable them to reinforce or confront their stereotypes? This may not be experienced by a White person, perhaps.

Any differences between a child's self-identity and how others identify them might create confusion in the child about their identity. Does visible likeness to the majority population, such as skin colour, enable a person to be identified as a White person? For example, Europeans may identify as belonging to the same race, but ethnicity may differ due to their cultural and linguistic differences. It is believed that as whiteness is 'invisible', and White people are a group that 'thrives on invisibility', they see their whiteness as an advantage and a shield against prejudice and discrimination (Gale, 2000, p.258). Colic-Peisker (2005) has referred to White Europeans enjoying 'advantageous self-identification' leading to 'self-inclusion'.

Cooper (2014) suggests that identity of a child is dynamic, that is, shaped by their experiences with their peers, parents/carers and teachers. Children negotiate, construct and reconstruct multiple identities that are multi-faceted. A range of social markers such as age, gender and ethnicity, family and group membership is used by children to determine their identity. A child's experiences will influence their identity and may change over time.

Brooker and Woodhead (2008) argued that the Western concept of identity as an individualised sense of self may not relate to the perceptions of identity recognised in different cultures. This idealised notion of individualised sense of self held by the practitioners in early childhood settings will impact on the experiences of children and families of migrants, refugees and asylum seekers due to the difference in the expectations of parents and settings. Practitioners and professionals are challenged to provide opportunities to all children irrespective of their backgrounds to develop a positive identity in early childhood settings. Children from migrant families have to make the effort to bridge two cultures and value systems. These children may be expected to adapt to the majority culture. Vandenbroeck (2008) warns against treating the culture of migrant children as fixed and static, as that might result in stereotypical and patronising attitudes. Further, he cautions practitioners against tokenistic practice in the early childhood settings, but rather ensuring that everybody is treated with respect. Providing positive opportunities will enable all children to develop a positive sense of identity.

Who can identify as British – what will be the acceptable criteria to classify oneself as British? Is it someone who is 'White' or who has been in the country for a certain length of time? What about a migrant whose family has been in the country for a few generations? What about a White person from Europe? Do people relate to their country or their religion to identify themselves or both?

## Reflection point

Are practitioners and/or teachers who are taking care of children aware of their diverse and changing needs? Can they relate to their social, emotional and cultural needs and are they able to empathise with their circumstances?

It is important for an individual to be accepted by their immediate and/or extended society to develop their self-esteem and sense of belonging. It is essential for a child, even a young child, to feel accepted, respected and included by others. As Farrell (2004) suggests, there are four conditions – presence, acceptance, participation and achievement – that should be met to fulfil inclusion of all children, irrespective of their abilities and backgrounds.

Identity relates to two dimensions – physical and psychological issues for an individual person. These can change and vary over time. Physical characteristics include physical changes, such as the impact of ageing on physical appearance, as well as what is visible. Psychological selves are regarded as the true identity that continues to remain unchanged through life. Garrett (1998) reported that some individuals may attempt to adapt their physical appearance as well as their personality to conform to expectations or what seems to be normal, but, fundamentally, their true identity may still remain inside them.

### Reflection point

What does the setting do to enable all children to be valued? How do they celebrate diversity and difference? How do children learn to respect everyone, irrespective of who they are and where they come from?

## INCLUSION IN PRACTICE

As a student on placement in an early childhood setting, make a list of resources that will provide positive images for children from diverse backgrounds.

An early childhood setting might stock a wide range of resources reflecting the diversity of the setting or the community. How are the resources used in the setting? Are children made aware of differences to enable them to respect these differences? Does the practitioner engage with the children and encourage them to discuss their opinions on the characters in a book or film? Do the children choose the books to read or resources to play? Do these books include characters that portray Black or non-White people in positive roles? Do practitioners have the knowledge and understanding to challenge their own stereotypes as well as those of the children and their families? Or do they reinforce these stereotypes by not discussing them?

## MIXED-RACE FAMILIES

The mixed-race population is one of the fastest-growing groups in the UK. There has been a steady increase in the number of children from mixed-race families. The concept of mixed race needs to be interpreted with a lot of caution as the definition is problematic. It may depend on how an individual identifies themselves, e.g. belonging to White, Black or mixed heritage, or White/Black Caribbean, White/Black African, White/Asian or any other mixed background. So, it is a challenge to establish an actual number. The 2011 Census (ONS, 2011a) shows that 45 per cent of children under 16 belong to a mixed-race background. Consequently, the number of children from mixed-race families in early childhood settings and schools is on the rise.

How do children relate to their identity if they belong to mixed heritage? Can these children relate to identifying themselves as White or Black or Asian? Is the identity of a child from a mixed-race family influenced by the dominant culture and the primary carer/parent, or by the presence or absence of one of the parents? For example, if a child's mother is English and their father is from Iran, and their father is travelling due to work commitments, will they be influenced by the mother's dominant presence and perhaps close proximity with their English grandparents? Might this result in the child preferring to identify as White? Sometimes the colour of the skin might be a big influence and other times the location of the child's home might also be responsible. A child might prefer to embrace an identity that might be of advantage. Young people experience tensions and contradictions relating to their own ethnic and cultural identities and how to relate to other ethnic minority groups. Do adults influence these tensions and conflicts unintentionally?

These children can be supported to develop their identity by providing access to a wide range of multicultural resources (stories, books, role play area) with positive images, respecting the traditions and beliefs of their families. It is important not to make assumptions about the child's abilities, and to communicate with the parents and grandparents, as well as the extended family (if feasible) of the child. Encourage parents to be involved in celebrating special events such as birthdays and festivals in the settings in the traditional ways they believe in. Respect all the children in the setting and offer a wide range of cultural experiences consistently. Provide learning activities that have cultural relevance to all children.

One Dear World,[1] a business run by a multicultural family consisting of Winnie, born and bred in Hong Kong, and Rafael, who is half-French, half-Greek, and their young son Alex, based in London, are 'on a mission to bring diversity and inclusion to young children'. They are engaged in producing a wide range of dolls that children can identify with. They hope to nurture global citizens through the dolls. They believe that 'all children, both boys and girls, deserve a doll that represents them so that they can develop a secure self-image. At the same time, seeing dolls that look different from them allows children to grow up

---

1    https://onedearworld.com

with a broad worldview and prepare them to make friends from around the world.'

Diversity Kids[2] is a Multicultural Consultancy Program based in Australia that provides unique inclusion support needs for educators and settings through a wide range of resources and ensures all children are valued. They actively work with settings, practitioners and diverse families and communities to instil positive perspectives of diversity to children from a young age.

## THEORETICAL BASE AND RESEARCH

The Office of National Statistics (ONS) (2001) in England and Wales referred to the following racial categories: White, mixed, Asian or Asian British, Black or Black British, or other White. They have introduced new categories, such as Middle East, English, Northern Irish, Scottish and Welsh, after criticism following the 2001 Census. Some additional categories such as the Gypsy, Roma and Traveller (GRT) tick-box under the 'White' heading and 'Arab' under the 'Other ethnic group' were added in 2011. However, some groups, such as Gypsies, Roma and Travellers, did not feel comfortable identifying themselves by ticking the specific box. It was reported that the 2011 Census reported only 58,000 people who identified as GRT living in England and Wales, and it was suggested that these figures may be underestimated (ONS, 2011c). This could be because 'Gypsies and Travellers continue to face high levels of racial discrimination, contributing to and exacerbating the inequalities they experienced' (Cromarty, 2019, p.11).

There is a lot of research around stages of racial awareness in young children and how it will influence their own identity. Goodman (1964) explained that children's racial awareness developed in three stages:

1. Phase 1: 2–3 years – racial awareness

---

2   www.diversitykids.com.au

2. Phase 2: 4–5 years – developing positive or negative orientation

3. Phase 3: 7–9 years – articulate their stereotypes and prejudices.

Is this theory still relevant in the contemporary context after 50 years? Cognitive development theorists believe that children's cognitive capacities influence how they perceive physical similarities and differences between people and develop racial attitudes (Levy *et al.,* 2004).

Davis, Leman and Barrett (2007) pointed to social developmental theorists who believed that children develop their racial identity in four phases:

1. Undifferentiated racial identity – children under three years old usually do not classify social groups based on who they are or based on their physical markers of race.

2. Racial awareness – children aged around three years notice and use physical markers to classify social groups and identify themselves.

3. Preference for one's groups – four-year-old children prefer to be with their own identity groups and compare different racial groups.

4. Prejudice against other groups – children aged seven dislike other groups, especially if they strongly identified with their groups and consider other groups are a threat.

However, MacNaughton and Davis (2009) challenged the idea that children are not capable of 'acting with racial intent' as they are believed to be 'ignorant and innocent' (p.2). They argued that 'Young children's ability and desire to use race, colour, to sort, classify, compare and assign status to people is a direct result of the politicizing of skin tone in a specific country or nation shape at a specific point and over time' (p.29). This is reinforced by Kinzler (2016), who opined that:

> by the time they start kindergarten, children begin to show many of the same implicit racial attitudes that adults in our culture hold. Children have already learned to associate some groups with higher status, or more positive value, than others.

### RACIAL AWARENESS OF CHILDREN

Consider the relevance of the research about children's racial awareness at different ages in the context of different countries and contemporary society. This can also be explored by discussing it with young children.

## THEY ARE NOT TOO YOUNG TO TALK ABOUT RACE

It is interesting to highlight research that reported children were aware of race at an earlier age, which is different to Goodman's theory discussed above. Children's Community School (Childrenscommunityschool.org, 2018) produced an infographic emphasising the early age at which young children can relate to race. The infographic has been produced based on the following, making references to a range of published research:

- At birth, babies look equally at the faces of all races. At three months, babies look more at faces that match the race of their caregivers (Kelly *et al.,* 2005).

- Children as young as two years use race to reason about people's behaviours (Hirschfeld, 2008).

- Expressions of racial prejudice often peak at ages four and five (Aboud, 2008).

- By 30 months, most children use race to choose playmates (Katz and Kofkin, 1997).

- By kindergarten, children show many of the same racial attitudes that adults in our culture hold – they have already learned to associate some groups with higher status than others (Kinzler, 2016).

- By five, Black and Latinx children in research settings show no preference toward their own groups compared to Whites; White children at this age remain strongly biased in favour of whiteness (Dunham, Baron and Banaji, 2008).

- Explicit conversations with five- to seven-year-olds about interracial friendship can dramatically improve their racial attitudes in as little as a single week (Bronson and Merryman, 2009).

Lee, Quinn and Pascalis (2017) report that racial bias begins at an early age – 6–9 months – as a result of not being exposed to people from different races. This finding challenges the perspective that racial bias emerges at three years of age. This is a result of their parents reinforcing stereotypical attitudes through their behaviour, overwhelming exposure to their own race and lack of exposure to people from other races, even through resources such as dolls, characters reflecting diverse backgrounds and races in books. Young children are not only influenced by who is around them, but also by who is not around.

It is often discussed what is the appropriate age to raise children's awareness about race. As racial awareness is developed at an earlier age, children can be exposed to positive images related to different categories of race and ensure stereotypes are not reinforced even at a very young age. Research by Heron-Delaney and colleagues (2011) found that when young babies are exposed to photos of people from different races, they are able to recognise and differentiate between different racial groups later in their lives.

Kelly *et al.* (2007) researched how faces observed within the visual environment affect the development of the face-processing system during the first year of life. They studied the ability of Caucasian infants (aged three months, six months and nine months) to discriminate faces from their own race and other racial groups (African, Middle-Eastern and Chinese). At three months, the infants are able to recognise all groups, at six months Caucasian and Chinese faces only, and at nine months, they were able to recognise only faces from their own race. This shows that awareness of other races seems to emerge at six months and is present at nine months. An influential research study was conducted in the 1930s by African American psychologists Clark and Clark (1939) in the USA. They studied racial awareness and self-identification in young children. Children aged six and nine years were asked to choose between a Black and a White doll when responding to these statements.

- 'Show me the doll that you like best or that you'd like to play with.'

- 'Show me the doll that is the "nice" doll.'

- 'Show me the doll that looks "bad".'

- 'Give me the doll that looks like a White child.'

- 'Give me the doll that looks like a coloured child.'

- 'Give me the doll that looks like a Negro child.'

- 'Give me the doll that looks like you.'

They investigated how children related to physical attributes such as skin tone, facial structure and hair type. The responses to the above questions suggested that the children represented White dolls positively irrespective of their skin colour. They reported that Black children chose White dolls when they were asked which dolls were nice, which dolls they would like to play with, and which were a nice colour. The children chose Black dolls when asked which dolls looked bad. This study reflected the hierarchy of different races in American society. Were these children aware of White supremacy in American society and how Black people were treated? Is this a result of being exposed to positive images of 'White' people in stories, books, media and television consistently?

After more than 80 years, have these perceptions been challenged and changed the perspectives of children, following the strong influences of Civil Rights activists, such as Martin Luther King, Rosa Parks and more recently ex-president Barack Obama?

Although this study was conducted in the USA and in the 1930s, the findings are relevant in the contemporary context as discrimination and stereotyping are still prevalent. CNN (2010) commissioned Beale Spencer to replicate this study and found that the same prejudices remained among White children, but African American children developed more positive attitudes towards the Black dolls. This test was replicated by Davis (2006) and found similar results to the original doll test in 1939. Another study by Byrd and colleagues (2017) examined 50 African American children's preference for dolls and reported that they did not want to look like the Black doll. However, there does seem to be a shift in the attitudes of Black children in their choice of White dolls over Black dolls. These studies indicate that, although there is a shift in the attitudes of Black children in developing positive feelings towards Black dolls, still their preferred choice of White dolls over Black dolls remains. These findings concur with Beale Spencer's view, quoted by CNN (2010), that 'we are still living in a society where dark things are devalued and white things are valued'.

Van Ausdale and Feagin (2001) indicated that when children use racist language, it may be because they are innocent and are not aware of the implications of using these words. Children are also assumed to imitate the language and behaviour of 'others' and not necessarily of close others, such as parents and/or carers. Children are considered to be 'cute or precocious' (p.4) when they show knowledge beyond their age and also when their behaviour is seen to be odd or naïve or unacceptable. Adults (parents as well as carers) interpret the children's use of language and behaviour in comparison to what they are expected to do rather than what they do. The authors also feel that 'adult whites learn to do racism – to think, feel and act in racist ways – within a social and historical context, while those who are not white learn that they must constantly contend with racial hostility and maltreatment in their everyday lives' (Van Ausdale and Feagin, 2001, p.31).

## LEGISLATION AND POLICY
### UNCRC

The United Nations Convention on the Rights of the Child (UNCRC) is an influential human rights treaty that promotes the rights of the child. Some of the articles relevant to race and ethnicity include:

► Article 2 (Non-discrimination): The Convention applies to all children, whatever their race, religion or abilities; whatever they think or say, whatever type of family they come from. It doesn't matter where children live, what language they speak, what their parents do, whether they are boys or girls, what their culture is, whether they have a disability or whether they are rich or poor. No child should be treated unfairly on any basis.

► Article 7 (Registration, name, nationality, care): All children have the right to a legally registered name, officially recognised by the government. Children have the right to a nationality (to belong to a country). Children also have the right to know and, as far as possible, to be cared for by their parents.

► Article 8 (Preservation of identity): Children have the right to an identity – an official record of who they are.

Governments should respect children's right to a name, a nationality and family ties.

► Article 22 (Refugee children): Children have the right to special protection and help if they are refugees (if they have been forced to leave their home and live in another country), as well as all the rights in this Convention.

## Equality Act 2010

In the UK, the Equality Act 2010 replaced all legislation related to discrimination with one single legislation. This law protects people from being discriminated against based on their gender, race, disability, religion or belief, or sexual orientation. This law prohibits direct discrimination, indirect discrimination, victimisation and harassment.

Implementing the Equality Act 2010 in schools and settings must relate to marketing of services provided, admission process, access to resources, an appropriate wide range of learning opportunities reflecting the diversity in the society, and acknowledging and respecting children and families from diverse backgrounds. The management of the setting must ensure all staff are provided with training opportunities to refresh their knowledge and understanding of the legislation and share good practice around how this legislation is interpreted and implemented in practice.

## ACTIVITY

The manager of an early childhood setting announces in the monthly meeting that they are expecting four new children:

• a two-year-old girl from Syria – an asylum seeker family

• a three-year-old boy from a Gypsy, Roma and Traveller family

- a three-and-a-half-year-old girl who speaks English as an additional language

- an 18-month-old boy from Australia.

The manager is discussing with all the staff members their strengths (knowledge and experiences of different cultures and languages) and implications for all of them in their individual roles to meet the needs of these children. The manager asks all the staff to note down their ideas on the specific and general needs of these children. What are their challenges and apprehensions about meeting the needs of these children? The setting wants the staff to help each other in ensuring all the children feel welcomed and to have settled down well and develop to the best of their potential.

What do we know about these children? Produce a poster sharing your ideas on their backgrounds, needs, families and resources (books, CDs, flags, household items, clothing, food, etc.) that might help them settle in.

## PRACTITIONERS

Meeting the needs of children from diverse families has been articulated to be a huge challenge by early childhood practitioners (Banerjee and Luckner, 2014). Practitioners from early childhood settings who work with children and families of diverse cultures, backgrounds and abilities may feel uncomfortable and may express a lack of confidence due to poor knowledge and understanding; they may lack specific knowledge, skills and competencies to meet the needs of children appropriately. Newly qualified teachers (NQTs) also highlighted their apprehensions to teach children from different ethnic backgrounds in NQT surveys consistently across several years. The number of NQTs who believed their training did not instil confidence in teaching children from diverse ethnic backgrounds is concerning (Devarakonda, McGrath and Chaudhary, 2019; Foley *et al.*, 2018). The NQT survey conducted every year since 2004 has been showing an increase in the numbers of NQTs who believed they were prepared and felt positive about the majority of criteria on the teacher training programme, apart from teaching children across all ethnic backgrounds, SEND pupils and EAL children.

Some practitioners might believe they can treat all children the same. This might result in practice influenced by stereotypes. Some children may have different needs compared to most children, due to their culture, language, food habits or medical needs, that practitioners might not be aware of. Practitioners may stereotype children from non-White and non-English-speaking families to have similar cultures. Practitioners can engage in open communication and dialogue with families to familiarise and clarify common knowledge as well as to redefine the stereotypes and prejudices about specific groups of people. It is important for practitioners to work in diverse contexts and be professional and empathetic towards all children and their families. Provide opportunities to children and parents to express themselves in diverse ways – verbal and nonverbal, face-to-face. They may not feel confident to speak in English due to their accent or competence in the English language. Parents and community members who are able to speak different languages could be encouraged to volunteer to help with interpreting and to bridge the communication gaps between the practitioners and parents.

Early childhood practitioners find engaging in conversation about race and racism with young children to be complex. Further, they find discussing this issue uncomfortable and sensitive. It was also found that the practitioners lack knowledge and understanding and appropriate resources to use with young children (Boutte, Lopez-Robertson and Powers-Costello, 2011; DCSF, 2009). Young children learn racist attitudes by observing adults' use of language and behaviours around them. A DECET and ISSA (2011) study explored the perceptions of experienced practitioners from different countries working with young children about the issues of diversity and equality. This study reported that, irrespective of their circumstances, qualifications, backgrounds and identities, they listed the following competencies as necessary for settings to address the equality and diversity issues:

- willing to accept diversity in society and respecting other ways of being

- being non-judgemental

- having an open mind

- having empathy and understanding

- showing flexibility and adaptability

- being sensitive (aware of children's and parents' needs) and responsive (act on this awareness)

- supporting a sense of belonging

- having enthusiasm: being engaged and motivated

- being creative in order to find alternative solutions and approaches

- showing warmth and being loving.

If children are not provided opportunities to formulate and question their initial understanding, it is likely that they will develop the rudiments of racism (Derman-Sparks, 2008). Earick (2008) believes a majority of White teachers from racially secluded areas did not experience any opportunities where different races are 'acknowledged, realised and processed' (p.341). Some teachers comment on the irrelevance of race or that it is not important in their setting due to lack of diversity. The presence of children from diverse backgrounds, as well as having appropriate resources, may not necessarily enable children to develop positive attitudes towards children from minority groups. It is important as a practitioner to be open and learn about what we do not know. Diversity is not only relevant in multicultural and multilingual early childhood settings, but also in monocultural settings.

## PRACTICE IN SETTINGS: GLOBE ACTIVITY ──────────

Settings can explore different countries around the world to enable children to raise their awareness, irrespective of whether children from different backgrounds are present in the setting. All children can explore their backgrounds and countries or places they originated from (with help from their practitioners and parents) on a globe and discuss/produce a collage.

- Where do I come from?

- What languages do they speak – how do they say 'hello', 'thank you', 'please'?

- What festivals and events do they celebrate?

- What and how do they eat?

- Let children choose a friend from any part of the world and explore their background.

## Adapting resources and books

The resources used in the early childhood settings did not reflect diversity found in the community; even if they did, references made in the books seem to reinforce stereotypical and negative messages (Crisp *et al.*, 2016).

In her blog, Park (2015) referred to an illustration titled 'Diversity in Children's Books 2015' by Huyck, Park Dahlen and Griffin, which highlight the lack of diversity in characters in children's books published in the USA. They reported that 73.3 per cent of characters are White, followed by 12.5 per cent animals, trucks, etc., 7.6 per cent Africans or African Americans, 3.3 per cent Asian Pacific/Asian Pacific Americans, 2.4 per cent Latinx and 0.9 per cent American Indians (see Huyck, Park Dahlen and Griffin, 2016).

A similar scenario has been reported in the children's books published in the UK (Flood, 2018). Arts Council England and the Centre for Literacy in Primary Education are also evaluating the extent of and quality of representation of characters from ethnic minority groups.

Teaching for Change[3] suggests that books for children must avoid stereotypes, discriminatory language, tokenism and negative judgements for specific groups. Encouraging children to be colour-blind may increase their biases to different races and limit their knowledge and understanding about diversity.

Practitioners can read the chosen story in advance to analyse the story for the following:

- characters – how the characters are defined, backgrounds of the characters, good or bad

- whether pictures are reinforcing stereotypes

- the language used

- storyline.

They could consider:

- customising the story to the local culture, context of the setting and individual children

- encouraging children to extend the story or change the ending of the story.

---

3   www.teachingforchange.org

## Culturally relevant pedagogy

Culturally relevant pedagogy (CRP) is an ideology that 'empower[s] students intellectually, socially, emotionally, and politically by using cultural references to impart knowledge, skills, and attitudes' (Grant and Ladson-Billings, 1997, p.18).

A teacher, irrespective of their racial or cultural origin, must have a conscious understanding of systemic inequities and structures that will influence and impact on the success and opportunities accessed by all children (Beauboeuf-LaFontant, 1999; Foster, 1990, 1997).

Tips to challenge discriminatory or biased comments from children:

1. Do not ignore a comment or question that is biased or discriminatory.

2. Respond immediately using language appropriate to the child's age and stage of development.

3. Do not penalise or ridicule the child's comments.

4. Ensure you correct the child with honest and accurate information.

5. Encourage children to access a wide range of resources from different contexts irrespective of their backgrounds.

## IMPACT OF STEREOTYPING AND PREJUDICE ON CHILDREN

The stereotypes and prejudices around race and ethnicity may lead to discrimination towards children and families. This discrimination might result in reduced or poor access to opportunities to develop appropriately. It will have an impact on the holistic development of the child, which might negatively influence their self-esteem. This in turn could prevent the child from performing to the best of their ability and thus the stereotype is reinforced. This cycle of discrimination will continue unless an intervention – in the form of a practitioner or a resource – is introduced that dispels stereotypes or prejudices and influences a change in the perspective or beliefs of practitioners and settings.

Figure 1.1 illustrates how individuals or early childhood settings may be actively engaging in racism unconsciously. On the other hand, practitioners can prevent racism by empowering, being proactive and educating themselves and others about diversity. This could be demonstrated through informal discussion with families and through research and provision of resources accessed from the internet, reading books and watching films from different countries and in different languages. It is important, especially if using information from external sources, to confirm with individual families that it is relevant and appropriate.

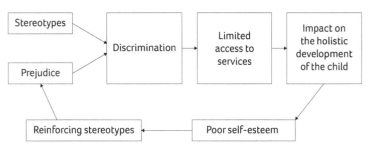

*Figure 1.1: The cycle of discrimination*

## WINDOW TO IDENTIFY PREJUDICES AND STEREOTYPES

As seen in the Introduction (see Figure I.3), this tool is adapted using the Johari Window model. This can be used by early childhood practitioners to reflect on their practice and establish their own prejudices and stereotypes related to children and families, as well as to practitioners belonging to minority groups. This tool helps enable them to understand their beliefs that might be influencing their stereotypes or prejudices held consciously or unconsciously.

All staff members can be included in an exercise encouraging them to discuss their prejudices and stereotypes and relate them to reality in small groups. Practitioners should discuss their backgrounds and culture directly with families, rather than make assumptions based on their limited knowledge and understanding. Henry (2016) believes that, as a sector, at times we don't feel comfortable discussing diversity issues for fear of 'getting it wrong' or 'offending'. We are comfortable discussing other important early years issues, but not diversity.

## Some key points from the chapter

× Early childhood professionals are expected to meet the evolving needs of children and their families from a wide range of contexts and backgrounds due to migration from different countries for a variety of reasons, including seeking asylum, fleeing from war-torn countries, moving to developed countries for higher education and better jobs, among others.

× The concept of race and ethnicity is constantly evolving, resulting in these terms being used interchangeably, synonymously or becoming redundant.

× References to an individual's own identity might differ over time and across generations. Further, there might be differences in how an individual perceives their own identity and how others identify them.

× Awareness of differences and having the appropriate knowledge and understanding and training will enable practitioners and policy makers to meet the needs of all children.

× The knowledge and understanding of all staff members can be updated by providing regular training to keep the practitioners confident about identifying and meeting the needs of all children. The resources in the setting should reflect the diversity of the setting, community and the country.

# 2

## Religion

This chapter will focus on:

- concepts of religious education and how these are evolving
- the shifts in religious affiliation
- theories influencing religious education (RE)
- conflict and controversies around emphasis on religious education in schools
- reflections and practice.

Traditionally and historically, childcare and education at all levels in the UK – primary, secondary and tertiary – was provided in faith-based settings, especially places of worship such as churches, and has been influenced by Christian values and beliefs. Educational settings have been significantly located around places of worship.

In the contemporary context, there is a need to increase awareness of differences and diversity related to religion, as well as non-religious worldviews. We need to prepare our children to acknowledge and accept people identifying with different religions and worldviews that they will be working with in the future. Children must be aware of the importance of valuing differences related to religious education and worldviews.

The concept of RE has changed over the years, reflecting changing perceptions. The Education Act 1944 mandated religion to be the base of the curriculum and it was referred to as Religious Instruction. The Education Reform Act 1988 initiated a change of subject name to Religious Education. Recently, the Religious Education Council of England and Wales set up an independent commission in 2016–2018 to review the current state of Religious Education in England. In 2018, the final report from the Commission on Religious Education recommended that the subject Religious Education be renamed to Religion and Worldviews to reflect the changing contexts of religion.

The term 'worldview' is a translation of the German word 'Weltanschauung', meaning a view of the world. 'A worldview is a person's way of understanding, experiencing and responding to the world – a philosophy of life. A person's worldview is likely to influence and be influenced by their beliefs, values, behaviours, experiences, identities and commitments' (CORE, 2018, p.4). Religious identity or affinity of individuals is on the decline and there has been a corresponding increase in awareness of and interest in the concept of worldviews, which may have resulted in the shift in terminology.

RE enables young people to recognise diverse religious and non-religious worldviews. This helps children to be prepared to live in a diverse society. On the other hand, some people felt that RE being compulsory for those children from families who didn't identify as religious was inappropriate. This influenced the shift from the concept of RE to worldview. Some people argued that the inclusion of RE in the curriculum may be pushing people to be religious (Jackson and Everington, 2017).

## STATISTICS

The UK Census (ONS, 2011a) showed that most of the population identified themselves as Christians; there were large communities of Muslims, Sikhs, Hindus and Jews, and smaller communities of Baha'is, Buddhists, Jains and Zoroastrians. Of the 56 million residents of England and Wales in 2011, 59 per cent were Christian, 5 per cent were Muslim, 0.4 per cent were 'Other' religion and 25 per cent had no religion. Almost half of the non-UK-born population identified as Christian (48%). This compares to 61 per cent of those born in the UK. Muslims were the second largest religion of the foreign-born population (19%). This compares to 3 per cent of the UK-born population. Around one in seven (14%) of the foreign-born population said they had no religion, compared to 27 per cent of those born in the UK. Table 2.1 shows the shift in religious identity revealed by comparing the censuses in 2001 and in 2011 England and Wales.

**Table 2.1: The 2001 and 2011 censuses**

| Religion | 2001 Census | 2011 Census |
|---|---|---|
| Christian | 72% | 59% |
| No religion | 15% | 25% |
| Muslim | 3% | 5% |
| Other religion | 3% | 4% |
| Not stated | 8% | 7% |

*Source: Census figures (ONS, 2001, 2011a)*

Another recent report quoted the Office of National Statistics (ONS) stating that the number of people who did not believe in any religion has almost doubled since 2011. Further, the number of people who identified with religions other than Christianity had increased, with 22 per cent identifying as Muslim, 17 per cent as Jewish and 13 per cent as Hindu (National Secular Society, 2019).

Ford, in an article in *The Times,* questioned if the shift in the increase in religious affiliation to minority religions was a result of migration and/or was due to an increase in the number of babies born to migrant mothers (Ford, 2019).

Britain is becoming more secular and tolerant of other religious beliefs. Sherwood reports that 'religious decline in Britain is generational; people tend to be less religious than their parents, and on average their children are even less religious than they are', and that 'faith has become private rather than institutional' (Sherwood, 2019). This suggests that younger people may be influenced by exposure to diverse religions from early childhood.

Hackett and Mcclenden (2017) from the Pew Research Center stated in their report that Christians are still the largest religious group in the world. However, the numbers are declining in Europe and Christians are an ageing population. This might mean that today's children will grow up in a diverse society with families identifying with diverse affiliations and different religions.

Reports also highlighted the increase in the population who do not identify with any religion (BBC, 2017; Sherwood, 2017). Further, those who did not identify with any religion may not associate with a specific religion, but they may have strong adherence to spirituality or a belief in god, a guiding force or subscribe to one of the other new wave of worldviews and beliefs such as humanism or Scientology.

It is also important to highlight that religious affiliation of the population has been inconsistent for Christianity across the world. While the number of people identifying as Christians in North America and Western Europe is on the decline, it is on the rise in the rest of the world. Bullivant (2018) conducted a survey of 16–29-year-olds about their religious affiliation in contemporary Europe. The findings indicated that a large proportion of young adults did not identify with any religion in the Czech Republic (91%), Estonia (80%), the UK (70%) and France (64%), while it is much lower in Israel (1%), Poland (17%) and Lithuania (25%). Further, it is interesting to consider if there is any relationship between people's identity with specific religions and their routines relating to their religion, such as praying, attending or engaging in religious rituals and services (whether it is in their own home or places of worship). Bullivant (2018) also reported that, increasingly, a large percentage of young adults never attend religious services and pray. What are the major issues influencing young people's beliefs and values related to their religious affiliation?

## RELIGION AND CURRICULUM

There are several countries around the world where faith of the child is one of the key admission criteria used in schools. Religion has influenced the provision of education in several countries. In the UK, several state schools are influenced by religious beliefs and values and are embedded in the curriculum and emphasised in daily rituals such as prayers in assembly and before lunch, special services related to key religious events around the year, and discussions and forums related to religious philosophy.

The Early Years Foundation Stage (DCSF, 2008) suggests providers must promote equality of opportunity and anti-discriminatory practice and must ensure that every child is included and not disadvantaged because of their ethnicity, culture or religion, home language, family background, learning difficulties or disabilities, gender or ability. The Early Years Foundation Stage (EYFS) framework is inclusive by meeting all children's needs. Practitioners are expected to encourage preschool children to explore and question differences related to majority and minority religious and belief systems. Role play areas can provide children with a wide range of resources related to different religions, such as clothes and symbols. The differences in cultures and religions can be discussed by sharing stories, listening to music, dancing, cooking and eating new foods. This will help children to learn that families are different, and appreciate and value the diversity of each other's lives. It is important for young children to approach early experiences related to religious education with open attitudes and interest and to feel free to discuss the place of religious experience in their own lives.[1]

In a positive learning environment, reference to cultural and religious diversity is encouraging and children can feel that they are able to express their viewpoints and beliefs in safety.

The EYFS strongly recommends that all planning and provision should be relevant to the child's experiences. It is vital that practitioners become aware of the individual child and the child's significant and unique experiences, in order that all activities and learning opportunities are appropriate to the needs of the child.

The new National Curriculum in England, introduced in 2014, offered to commit to each 'pupil's spiritual and cultural development' (Department for Education (DfE), 2014a). Following a review, a new curriculum is being developed for schools in Wales for implementation from 2020, suggesting that 'diversity of religion and belief will also be valued highly in the new framework' (Welsh Government, 2018; see also Hemming, Hailwood and Stokes, 2018).

## CURRICULUM AND QUALIFIED TEACHERS

In the UK, one-third of schools are religious. There are a wide range of schools influenced by diverse religious beliefs, including the Churches of England and Wales, Roman Catholic, Jewish, Muslim, Hindu and Sikh. According to the guidance from the DfE document Schools Admissions Code, all schools are expected to take 50 per cent of children based on the religion or religious denomination and the other 50 per cent to be not influenced by faith (DfE, 2014c).

Strangeways-Booth's (2017) report quoted a DfE spokesman who said that religious education is compulsory at all key stages

---

1   References to RE are relevant to the latter part of the EYFS, i.e. older children (3–5 years); it is taught formally from Key Stage 1 (ages 5–7).

and is expected to 'actively promote mutual respect and tolerance of those with different faiths and beliefs'. But it has been revealed that more than a quarter of schools do not offer RE (Strangeways-Booth, 2017). It has been reported that unqualified teachers taught RE unlike other subjects (Syal, 2017). Further, the quality of RE provision is not consistent across different key stages and schools. According to the National Association of Teachers of Religious Education (NATRE) (2019), Ofsted does make references to religious education in their general comments relating to the quality of the curriculum. But it does not specifically consider RE provision when monitoring the quality of a school and there are no specific targets related to attainment in RE provision. Further, the National Curriculum allows parents to opt their children out of RE lessons and related study trips. This means that RE is now considered to be a non-academic subject and an option that is not prioritised. Although RE is compulsory at every key stage of school, there is no nationally agreed curriculum, so it varies according to local authority in England.

The Religious Council of England and Wales (REC) (2018) flagged up to a 'chronic shortage' of qualified RE teachers. The Government School Workforce Survey (DfE, 2016) reports that 55 per cent of RE teachers do not possess a qualification above A level in the subject. Sellgreen (2018) warns that the shortage of teachers could result in school pupils being ignorant and might reinforce stereotyping and discrimination based on faith and religion. Schools are struggling not only to recruit but also to retain RE teachers. Sellgreen quoted the Head of Religious Education at a school in the East Midlands, who highlighted that the 'dynamic ever-changing society full of different perspectives, beliefs and cultures' might require the school pupils to be prepared, so that 'learning about these things helps the pupils' and 'helps them develop a genuine understanding about the world and the people in it' that will help them to 'shape the society of the future'.

## RELIGION IN PRACTICE

A 2006 report from the Department for Education and Skills (DfES, 2006), based on research with a sample of 15,450 school students, revealed that 55 per cent of Indians (Hindu, Sikh and Muslim), 71 per cent of Black Africans (predominantly Christian but also Muslim) and 85 per cent of Pakistani and Bangladeshis (almost all Muslim) held religion to be very important to their way of life, and a significant additional number in these and other ethnic groups assigned to it a 'fairly important role'.

There are several ways to provide inclusive and non-discriminatory practice in early childhood settings and schools. Knowledge and understanding can be developed through:

- raising awareness of different routines related to religious festivals observed by practitioners and parents through discussion of their own faith and beliefs; this enriches knowledge and understanding related to differences in perceptions related to faiths and beliefs

- ensuring that all staff attend training to extend their knowledge and understanding of equality and diversity

- sharing practices and values about faith and the belief systems of families to extend knowledge and understanding

- considering what impact practitioners' knowledge and understanding of different religions and festivals will have on the experiences of children in a setting.

Early childhood settings should:

- develop and review policies around inclusion and diversity on a regular basis

- ensure that an equal opportunity policy will celebrate and value the diverse religious, cultural and non-religious beliefs and practices of families and staff

- ensure that all staff attend training to extend their knowledge and understanding of equality and diversity

- ensure that the preparation and provision of all food in the setting is meeting the dietary restrictions of families, children and staff, such as halal, vegetarian, vegan and kosher foods

- be alert to the need to avoid racial, cultural and gender stereotyping.

## ACTIVITIES AROUND FESTIVALS AND CELEBRATIONS IN THE SETTING

- Organise coffee mornings and discussions with parents to create informal opportunities to share information about celebrations and festivals related to different religions and worldviews. Faith and non-faith groups can be brought together from the wider community to encourage respect and understanding of diversity.

- Plan festivals with the children, practitioners/teachers and families to provide a broad range of experiences. Do not ignore important local festivals. Organise activities focusing on food, encouraging and sharing dishes related to festivals from different cultural and religious traditions at festivals and events.

- Ensure festivals are celebrated at the appropriate time of year to help children to make sense of the experiences, beliefs and values related to the festival.

- Ensure the setting focuses on a range of festivals and celebrations related to different religious and non-religious groups reflecting the diversity in the community.

- Ensure the activities are appropriate to the age of

the children. Consider giving holistic experience by relating to a wide range of experiences related to the festival – cultural, social, creative. Read stories related to the festival and which describe the significance of celebrating the festival. Practitioners and faith community representatives should be careful that they are clear about the level at which they should approach these areas with young children.

- Whole school assemblies and RE lessons could provide children with opportunities to explore religious dietary restrictions to clarify any misconceptions and confusion regarding specific needs, e.g. halal food for Muslims, kosher for Jewish, strict vegan/vegetarian diets for certain Hindus.

Consider the following questions to plan and organise a festival calendar:

- Are there any children or staff of different faith groups in your setting? If not, how will this festival be celebrated? When is this festival celebrated?

- How does this fit into your planning over the year?

- What will the children gain from this experience?

- How will you involve staff, children, parents/carers and community leaders?

- What stories are relevant? How can the stories be simplified to the child's level? What resources will be used to support the story?

- What key activities/experiences/opportunities should be used to extend the story?

- Will this activity be repeated?

- How will this activity be adapted to different key stages?

## AUDIT OF FESTIVALS AND CELEBRATIONS: DISCUSSION BETWEEN PRACTITIONERS AND CHILDREN

How many festivals do you celebrate in the setting? List them.

Which religion/s do these festivals relate to?

List the key features related to these festivals. What is the significance of these festivals?

How do the children in your setting celebrate Christmas? Are there differences in the traditions, values, rituals and expectations related to Christmas? Discuss.

What aspects of Christmas do children enjoy most and which are least liked? Is this list different to that of staff members?

Make a list of religions and worldviews that children and their families in the setting believe in.

Produce a collage of information, photos and pictures related to different festivals.

Christmas might be celebrated differently by families within national and international contexts. While for some families the emphasis is on engaging in religious activities such as worshipping and attending church, others might see it as an opportunity for family reunion, or just an occasion to meet to exchange gifts. The religious rituals will be influenced by local culture and social expectations. The practitioner/teacher could encourage all children to share their experiences of the celebrations related to Christmas with their families and discuss how they differ in the small group in the class. This will raise lots of interesting issues related to the nature and contexts of differences in the celebrations and what the key influences are. Parents and grandparents may also be invited to join, which may result in enriched discussion about the intergenerational differences in the values and traditions related to Christmas.

By learning about festivals in different religions, the aim is to promote harmony and sense of respect among the community members. Families play an important role in celebrating festivals. Christmas is celebrated in different ways, influenced by local cultures (e.g. the local traditions and customs influence the celebrations in England, Spain, China and India) and seasons (e.g. Finland, Australia). Some festivals are celebrated to welcome different seasons, the new year, share harvest, honouring ancestors and to celebrate the birthdays of gods. People visit places of worship, feast or fast at different festivals and prepare and share special food, exchange gifts, wear new clothes, narrate stories and play music and dance together. A poster can be produced in collaboration with parents and community members to reflect the values and beliefs behind the celebrations, rituals and activities.

Table 2.2 contains information about some Hindu festivals, including the activities and experiences children and families are engaged in celebrating together.

**Table 2.2: Profile of Hindu religious festivals**

| Name of festival | When it is celebrated | Significance | Key activities/ experiences |
|---|---|---|---|
| Holi (festival of colours) | Spring (March) | Onset of Spring | People visit family, friends and foes and throw or put coloured powders on each other, laugh and gossip, share food and drinks and enjoy music (everyone in the community, irrespective of age, socioeconomic status, gender or religion, participates) |

| New year – Baisakhi, Ugadi, Gudi Padwa | Spring (March/ April) | To celebrate the new year according to the Hindu calendar | Decorating indoors and outdoors with colourful patterns, rich food<br><br>Celebrations differ according to the cultures of local communities |
|---|---|---|---|
| Rakhi or Rakshabandhan (bond of protection) | August | Strengthen the bonds of love and relationship between a brother and sister | Sisters tie a string around their (elder and younger) brother's wrist and receive a gift in return and promise to support each other |

This table can be adapted for other religions, as well as non-religious celebrations, by discussing them with children and their families, including parents and grandparents, community groups and practitioners in the settings. This activity will encourage children in the setting to relate to the diversity of festivals and celebrations and respect everyone for their uniqueness. Children should know and understand about their own culture and beliefs and those of other people; that there are differences between people and that this does not mean some practices are superior and others inferior. Children should know and understand the symbolism behind the rituals which are part of everyday life. Some of these rituals could be religious and others cultural.

## A COLLAGE ON RELIGION

Fill in the table below and produce a collage on religion and review regularly to update or add new information. This collage can be informed and filled by practitioners, children and their families.

**Table 2.3: Information on religious diversity in an early childhood setting**

| Name of religion | Signs external and visible | Religious book | Place of worship | Key beliefs | Origins | Rituals | Festivals and celebrations |
|---|---|---|---|---|---|---|---|
| Christianity | | | | | | | |
| Islam | | | | | | | |
| Hinduism | | | | | | | |
| Judaism | | | | | | | |
| Sikhism | | | | | | | |

A setting can choose to include festivals relevant to their setting and community. This collage can be displayed in the setting to raise awareness about different religions.

## CIRCLE TIME ACTIVITY

Discuss daily routines with children and include persona dolls representing a child from a new religion. This will enable the children to share their ideas about why certain rituals are part of everyday life and their values (e.g. washing hands before meals). Children need to be aware and understand that some of the rituals can be different in their individual lives that might have a different symbolic outlook and religious meaning. These symbols could relate to religion and/or faith or culture of their communities, and provide opportunities to talk about everyday routines that we perform as individuals or in groups, for example bedtime rituals or family prayers. Discuss rituals associated with festivals, including foods and personal stories about getting ready for festivals/individual family celebrations. A positive stance from the practitioner and/or teacher will be proactive in exploring the individual child's home cultures and to reflect the diversity in the local and national communities.

## RESEARCH ACTIVITY

From the perspectives of different majority religions, research the following:

- dress and uniform code

- food relating to religion

- external symbols and important features of the religions.

## LEGISLATION AND POLICY

The Equality Act 2006 defines religion as any religion and religious or philosophical belief. This includes all the major religions, as well as less widely practised ones. Belief is a difficult concept to define as it is evolving and broadening all the time and may include beliefs such as atheism and humanism. The European Court of Human Rights has ruled that 'a belief must be more than merely an opinion or idea. It must attain a level of cogency, seriousness, cohesion and importance, must be worthy of respect in a democratic society and must not be incompatible with human dignity' (HM Government, 2010). The Equality Act 2010 sets out provisions to protect individuals against discrimination on grounds of religion or belief (including lack of religion or belief) when goods, facilities and services are being provided. The Equality Act 2010 defines religion and belief in the following way:

1. Religion means any religion and a reference to religion includes a reference to a lack of religion.

2. Belief means any religious or philosophical belief and a reference to belief includes a reference to a lack of belief. (p.10)

The Equality Act 2010 advocates that schools must not discriminate admission of children based on religion or belief. Section 2.8 of the School Admissions Code states:

With the exception of designated grammar schools, all maintained schools, including faith schools, that have enough places available must offer a place to every child who has applied for one, without condition or the use of any oversubscription criteria. (DfE, 2014c, p.22)

The following are the specific articles from UNCRC (UNICEF, 1989) that encourage children to access their rights related to their religion:

▶ Article 9 of the European Convention of Human Rights: Everyone has a right, in public and private, to manifest his (or her) religion or belief.

▶ Article 14 (freedom of thought, conscience and religion): Children have the right to think and believe what they want and to practise their religion, as long as they are not stopping other people from enjoying their rights. Parents should help guide their children in these matters. The Convention respects the rights and duties of parents in providing religious and moral guidance to their children. Religious groups around the world have expressed support for the Convention, which indicates that it in no way prevents parents from bringing their children up within a religious tradition. At the same time, the Convention recognises that as children mature and are able to form their own views, some may question certain religious practices or cultural traditions. The Convention supports children's right to examine their beliefs, but it also states that their right to express their beliefs implies respect for the rights and freedoms of others.

▶ Article 30 (children of minorities/indigenous groups): Minority or indigenous children have the right to learn about and practise their own culture, language and religion. The right to practise one's own culture, language and religion applies to everyone; the Convention here highlights this right in instances where the practices are not shared by the majority of people in the country.

## Fundamental British Values

In England, schools are also expected to promote 'Fundamental British Values'. These values include 'democracy, the rule of law, individual liberty, and mutual respect for and tolerance of those with different faiths and beliefs and those without faith' (Ofsted, 2017, p.40).

The official guidance on Fundamental British Values (Department for Education, 2014b) states that pupils should develop 'an understanding that the freedom to choose and hold other faiths and beliefs is protected in law' (p.6), as well as 'an acceptance that other people having different faiths or beliefs to oneself (or having none) should be accepted and tolerated, and should not be the cause of prejudicial or discriminatory behaviour' (p.6).

Eaude (2018) believed these Fundamental British Values (FBV) were expected to be actively promoted by schools in response to the 'rise of radicalisation' (p.67). Schools expressed an inability to demonstrate that they were actively promoting Fundamental British Values. Eaude also referred to philosophical problems in interpreting Fundamental British Values. He questioned the references made to Britishness, especially 'for those who are not British-born, or may be perceived not to be, and whose religion and culture may lead to their Britishness being open to question'.

Van Krieken Robson (2019) referred to the 'British' in Fundamental British Values as problematic and complex (p.101). Practitioners complied with the expectations of engaging with Fundamental British Values through public displays of symbols associated with national identity, such as the British flag, the Queen's head and Union Jack, that were considered patriotic and nationalistic. Lockley-Scott (2019) suggests that these symbols might 'become conflated with nationalism or patriotism rather than being understood as a set of positive guidelines for living together as a society' (p.364). Some teachers worry about how to teach British values in a classroom with diverse pupils (Maylor, 2016) and question the relevance of these symbols to children and their families with diverse histories, nationalities and ethnicities.

Maylor (2010) believed that teachers may not have a good understanding of the backgrounds of pupils from ethnic minority groups who were considered to be immigrants rather than British. Maylor (2016) raised an important question about Britishness – is it related to being White? She argued that the 'emphasis on fundamental British values in teaching and teacher education is… justified as they are considered central to the moulding of a British identity' (p.318). She also warned about teacher educators' ability to prepare teachers effectively to promote British values.

## Prevent Strategy

The Prevent Strategy (HM Government, 2011) was launched in 2007 and reviewed in 2011. The focus of the Prevent Strategy is to prevent terrorism and to build resilience in children. HM Government has produced the Prevent Strategy to ensure the UK is made a safer place for everyone by engaging with diverse community groups. It expects all schools and registered childcare providers to 'have due regard to the need to prevent people from being drawn into terrorism'. This is called the Prevent duty. One of the guiding principles of the Prevent Strategy is: 'Prevent will also mean intervening to stop people moving from extremist groups or from extremism into terrorist-related activity' (HM Government, 2011, p.6).

The Prevent Strategy has attracted criticism from many quarters, including Muslim organisations. For example, An-Nisa Society considered the Prevent Strategy to be 'flawed and fraught with perils' (Kahn, 2009, p.3) as Muslim communities were disproportionately criminalised. The negative stereotypes of Muslims as terrorists were reinforced. This led to Muslim communities falling under the media spotlight and attracting the attention of far-right groups. This resulted in some Muslims, especially women and children, choosing to socially exclude themselves. Terrorist incidents in different parts of the world have been reported to be organised by fundamental Muslim organisations, which has influenced people to develop a fear of

Muslims (Islamophobia), and the media has reinforced these perceptions.

Versi (2017) expressed his concern about the number of Muslims referred under the Prevent duty in 2016. He reported that one in 500 Muslims was referred to Prevent in 2016. Grierson (2019) reported that families and children were terrified of having discussions about religion for fear of being misunderstood and children were worried about practising their religion in schools, as it can result in being wrongly referred under the Prevent duty. This is having a negative impact on children.

## Theoretical base

Moulin-Stożek and Metcalfe (2018) explore the transition of Religious Education (RE) in England and Wales from single-faith society to multi-faith and identified three moral approaches for the multi-faith religious education:

- The universalist approach emphasises the same morals of different religions.

- The vicarious approach focuses on the moral teachings and practices supporting the religious worldviews.

- The instrumentalist approach relates to the need to study different religions to enable children to develop their competence and knowledge to live in a multi-faith society in harmony.

Ipgrave (2010) described two different types of inclusion in English schools: identity-based inclusion and epistemology-based inclusion. The first model relates to questions of 'who I am', and the second with 'how I understand reality'. Identity-based inclusion aims to reduce discrimination based on ethnicity and to encourage celebration of cultural diversity in the school, enabling all children to achieve the best of their abilities. There are two perspectives related to an identity-based approach: permissive inclusion and affirmative inclusion (Ipgrave, 2010). Permissive inclusion allows pupils to show their religious identity within schools, without any barriers. Affirmative methods are limited by teachers' choices and perceptions, and are therefore not fully inclusive. The second model is epistemology-based inclusion, which should encourage children to show how religion influences them to express what they think and say and not be just explicit in what they wear and eat.

Jackson (2009) proposed an interpretive approach to understand traditions around different religions and to increase the knowledge and understanding of all children. Three concepts have been used to analyse religious diversity:

- Representation of religion relates to diversity of people in their own context and culture from the perspective of tradition, group and individual.

- Interpretation relates to comparing and contrasting the familiar and unfamiliar concepts in different religions.

- Reflexivity allows children to relate to the impact of learning about new religions on their own values and views.

Ipgrave (2015) discussed the importance of providing opportunities for children to express their views on plurality. She refers to three levels of dialogue with children:

1. primary – acceptance of plurality

2. secondary – being open to difference

3. tertiary – pupil interaction.

From the perspective of teachers, she suggested three themes:

1. children's narrow understanding of diversity

2. intergenerational dialogue between generations to relate to the traditions actively rather than passively

3. opportunities to share knowledge and best practice with other teachers.

Theories discussed provided a foundation for settings to justify the references made to religion and non-religious perspectives to raise awareness among children. The early childhood settings and schools could implement these perspectives to encourage inclusion of religion and beliefs into the school routines.

## DEBATES AND CONTROVERSIES AROUND RELIGION IN EDUCATIONAL SETTINGS

Young children face challenges when they attend an early childhood setting or school where they must adhere to and meet different expectations. These challenges can relate to: use of visible and external symbols, inconsistent expectations between home and school, dress codes – covering the head or wearing a swimming costume or shorts for PE/games, food and dietary restrictions, and adhering to the specific restrictions placed by settings or homes. Some parents' and families' expectations about dress codes might conflict with the dress codes children are expected to adhere to at school. For example, there have been media reports about schools banning headscarves (C. Turner, 2017).

The low status some schools ascribe to religious education is evident with unqualified teachers engaged in teaching RE and parents withdrawing children from attending RE lessons by choice, as discussed earlier in the chapter.

### Food and dietary restrictions

Some religions may recommend avoiding some food and drinks

and/or require food to be prepared and consumed in a specific manner. Some schools may wish to provide vegetarian, halal and kosher options through the school lunch service to cater to the needs of Hindu, Sikh, Muslim and Jewish pupils. However, it may be worthwhile ensuring that the specific individual dietary needs of the children are clarified, rather than basing provision on stereotyped assumptions, as it might also depend on individual health needs and/or allergies. Such approaches can provide valuable learning opportunities for children and may help build connections between the school and the wider community.

Some restrictions, such as halal (Islam) or kosher (Judaism) food, are imposed by religious guidelines and some are the personal choices of families.

## Dress codes

Children experience difficulties due to conflicts in the expectations of parents, schools and peers. Children often struggle to decide whether to conform to the norms of society or adhere to the values and traditions of their family's cultural expectations. For some women identifying with Islam, wearing headscarves can be an important aspect of their identity development (Wilson, 2015). Recently there were reports about pupils being prevented from wearing their headscarf to school. R. Turner (2017) reported the case of a Catholic school banning a four-year-old from wearing a headscarf and expecting parents to 'respect their strict uniform policy'. Conflicts related to the dress codes of older girls are more common, but it is unusual to find a report about a dress code involving a four-year-old.

Skirt-length for girls can also be a controversial issue. Dress code policies for girls can be a matter of concern to parents and families who strongly believe that their religious and cultural beliefs do not permit girls to wear certain dresses (e.g. short skirts, swimwear or shorts for PE/games or sports). There are tensions between children and their families around meeting the different (sometimes conflicting) expectations of parents and schools and also peer pressure on children to conform to the norms and expectations of their society.

Children can be bullied if they do not conform to their peers and are sometimes pressured to conform by the settings. The Childline website has advice for children on faith and religious bullying.[2] It states that some of the reasons for this bullying include their affiliation to religion and religious practices related to not eating meat or drinking alcohol and wearing visible faith symbols (e.g. headscarf, cross, non-Western clothes).

## Some key points from the chapter

× The population of the UK is evolving and the demographics and belief systems of the population are changing. Although the majority of the population identify as Christians, their perspectives and practices in relation to rituals, such as attending church every Sunday or offering prayers, may be on the decline.

× Religion was historically an important feature of the curriculum across different key stages of education – primary to tertiary level. In recent years, religious education has been taught by unqualified teachers.

× The recent shift in values related to religion in education is to ensure that children and young people are aware of the beliefs around different religions and worldviews and can accept and respect each other and are prepared to live in a diverse society.

---

2   www.childline.org.uk/info-advice/bullying-abuse-safety/types-bullying/faith-religious-bullying

× The context of education has moved away from being heavily influenced by Christian beliefs and values to a greater emphasis on other religions and worldviews.

× Terror-related incidents are influencing policies and initiatives in the UK. The Government introduced the Prevent Strategy that prevents radicalisation and enforces all educational settings to promote Fundamental British Values.

# 3

## Culture

This chapter will focus on:

- perceptions of the concept of culture

- theories related to culture

- good practice of culture in early childhood settings

- challenges and debates related to culture

- references to theory, legislation and policy.

All children, families and practitioners/teachers should be able to feel proud of their cultures relating to their backgrounds, traditions, beliefs and values. Nowadays, multiculturalism is seen in societies around the world due to permeable boundaries between countries and regions.

How is culture perceived? Does culture differ from one family to another, one generation to another, one region to another in the same country? What are the reasons for the dynamic nature of culture? The changing nature of culture in diverse contexts has raised concerns about the quality of experiences of children from different backgrounds. Is it feasible for practitioners and settings to meet the diverse needs of a wide range of children belonging to different cultures?

Culture is a multi-faceted concept, wide and fuzzy, complicated. Culture is dynamic, irrespective of what culture an individual or community is part of. While change is expected, cultural roots need to be valued and respected.

> Culture appears to have become key in our interconnected world, which is made up of so many ethnically diverse societies, but also riddled by conflicts associated with religion, ethnicity, ethical beliefs, and, essentially, the elements which make up culture. (Rossi, quoted by Zimmerman, 2017)

Conflicts and misunderstandings between people might be a result of ignorance or of not valuing the traditions and beliefs of others. In the context of early years education, there can be a mismatch between settings/practitioners and those children and their families belonging to minority cultures.

## Reflection points

How do you ensure children are valued? Give examples from your setting.

What resources are available in your setting/school that represent different cultures positively?

## DEFINITIONS

Find some definitions of culture below. Discuss how these definitions have changed across time and geographical boundaries. What are the key differences?

> A culture is a configuration of learned behaviors and results of behavior whose component elements are shared and transmitted by the members of a particular society. (Linton, 1945, p.32)

Kroeber and Kluckhohn (1952) summarised various definitions of culture as:

Culture consists of patterns, explicit and implicit, of and for behavior acquired and transmitted by symbols, constituting the distinctive achievements of human groups, including their embodiments in artifacts; the essential core of culture consists of traditional (i.e. historically derived and selected) ideas and especially their attached values; culture systems may, on the one hand, be considered as products of action, and on the other as conditioning elements of further action. (p.181)

Culture can be a set of fundamental ideas, practices and experiences of a group of people that are symbolically transmitted generation to generation through a learning process. Culture may as well refer to the beliefs, norms, and attitudes that are used to guide our behaviours and solve problems. (Chen *et al.*, 1998, p.25)

Siraj-Blatchford (1994, pp.28–29) points out:

culture, like language, is dynamic and ever changing. Our parents pass on their culture to their children but they do it through vehicles such as language, play, art and literature. Schools and other educational institutions extend our learning in this way through humanities, science, the arts, etc. Our culture also determines what clothes we wear, our diet, religious beliefs and relationships. Culture is much more than this, but the important point is that it is learnt and that it is all around us.

Rossi, an anthropologist (quoted in Zimmerman, 2017), defined culture as follows:

Culture encompasses religion, food, what we wear, how we wear it, our language, marriage, music, what we believe is right or wrong, how we sit at the table, how we greet visitors, how we behave with loved ones, and a million other things.

## Reflection point

Why do some cultures change drastically while others tend to preserve their traditions and values more than others? Are some cultures considered to be superior or valued more than others? Is there any impact of colonising on the spread of Western cultures? Does the value we place on the dominant culture reinforce its sense of superiority and higher value compared to the cultures of minority groups?

## TYPES OF CULTURES

There is a wide range of cultures around the world. Cultures are different based on location and ethnic and linguistic backgrounds. Cultures vary – some encourage being individualistic, others collectivistic. Individualistic cultures emphasise uniqueness, independence and individual interests. Western culture encourages individualistic attributes. Other cultures are broadly influenced by collectivistic cultures, as they relate to their social context, to achieve social harmony.

### Western culture

The term 'Western culture' relates to European countries, as well as those that have been heavily influenced by European immigration, such as America, Australia, New Zealand, Canada and South Africa, where English is a majority language. The influence of Western culture is widespread around the world.

### Eastern culture

Eastern culture refers to the societal norms of countries in Far East Asia (including China, Japan, Vietnam, North Korea and South Korea) and the Indian subcontinent. Eastern culture emphasises social norms, values, traditions, customs, belief systems, political systems, and specific artefacts and technologies.

## Latin American culture

Latin culture is dominant in many of the Spanish-speaking nations including Mexico and those in Central America and South America, influenced by Spanish or Portuguese culture and languages.

## Middle Eastern culture

Middle Eastern culture refers to approximately 20 countries in the Middle East. The culture is mainly influenced by language and religion. Arabic is the commonly spoken language, with a wide variety of dialects, although religion is a common cultural thread in all these countries.

## African culture

African culture is the basis for all cultures as humans originated on this continent and migrated to other areas of the world around 60,000 years ago. Africa is a big continent with a rich culture that influenced other cultures and has also been influenced by other cultures. For example, Ubuntu is an African philosophy and popular concept that emphasises the importance of relationships between people and is often translated as 'I am because we are'.

## GOOD PRACTICE ───────────────────────

As an early childhood settings manager, encourage all practitioners to locate their place of origin on a geographical map. Share their knowledge of culture (including their own) in their own local area to a wider region. Discuss if there are any practices or traditions that are unique and/or influenced by other cultures. Make a list of traditions and practices related to common events such as birthdays, religious festivals and celebrations – Christmas, Eid, Diwali, Hanukkah, Thanksgiving.

## THEORIES OF CULTURE

Some practitioners believe that they are inclusive by celebrating a few different festivals with display posters, and including a variety of clothes, articles and artefacts from different cultures in the role play area. When a child asks questions about the name of an article or dress, the purpose of this article or the circumstances in which clothes are worn, the practitioner may be unsure. This practice might sound tokenistic.

Is it feasible or possible for practitioners to become bicultural? Klug and Whitfield (2003) suggested that individuals – children and adults (parents and practitioners) – placed themselves on a continuum as traditional, bicultural and assimilated (modern) based on their experiences of diversity.

Traditional ◄————► Bicultural ◄————► Assimilated

Klug and Whitfield (2003) made references to children from the perspective of the culture of American Indian families. They believed that children and families were traditional, bicultural and assimilated based on the influences of their elders and also the wider society in which they lived and how they were raised. They suggested that a person can place themselves anywhere on this line as a continuum. This can be relevant to anyone belonging to any culture and in any part of the world. It depends on how much an individual is exposed to major cultures and needs to relate to people outside the home, for example due to attending school or work, or other reasons to move on the continuum.

A child, family or practitioner can be classed as traditional if they have been strictly raised with their cultural norms and with minimum exposure to other cultures. Those children who are brought up by their grandparents may be traditional as a result of limited exposure to the dominant culture in addition to the consistent reinforcement of values instilled from their own culture. They might strongly believe in their cultural practices and may resist from adapting to new cultural expectations. A bicultural teacher or a child may be aware of practices from both cultures. They are able to switch between their own culture and the new culture comfortably. A child or adult may decide to be traditional or bicultural in different contexts.

Individuals who are bicultural are familiar with their own culture and also the majority culture. They might be able to code switch between cultures and two or three languages. They are able to understand the expectations of both cultures related to behaviour, dress, food, values, etc. They are bicultural by being actively involved in their own culture as well as adhering to and being able to adapt to the norms of the majority culture.

An individual who feels that they have assimilated might feel nominally attached to their own cultural heritage or, in some extreme cases, they might not feel comfortable with or even resist being referred to as belonging to their own culture. They might show their preference to the majority culture, especially with their values, behaviour and ways of thinking, in an explicit manner. It depends on the number of years they are exposed to another culture and how much they would like to be included by the mainstream community.

An assimilated person is one who has totally embraced the new cultural values and expectations. People who are categorised like this are usually out of touch with their own culture. Physically, they may appear to be like an Asian or African in an English society, but their values and attitudes may reflect the dominant culture's way of thinking. Individuals may prefer not to be identified as belonging to a minority community. It was also presumed that people belonging to the majority culture and those with fair skin were superior, and this may perhaps explain why some people prefer to belong to the superior group and seek to be accepted by their peers belonging to the majority culture.

Is an immigrant expected to be familiar with the cultural norms of the new culture after moving to a new country? Absorbing relevant aspects of another culture is complicated. Some individuals might feel uncomfortable understanding and relating to the new culture. These children and their families might benefit from the setting supporting them by acknowledging and valuing the minority culture and encouraging them to share it with others, as well as being made familiar with the expectations and norms of the majority culture. Despite belonging to a minority culture and living in another country, an individual might feel comfortable with their own beliefs and cultural practices. They can influence and also be influenced by the explicit and visible expectations and values related to the majority culture.

What about children from mixed marriages – would they adopt the dominant and superior culture? Are these children in any danger of being excluded from mainstream activities irrespective of their cultural orientation because of their appearance?

## Six stages to becoming a bicultural teacher

Practitioners and teachers have a responsibility to provide quality education to all children irrespective of their background, culture, etc. An awareness of different cultures will enable them to provide appropriate care relevant to all children's needs. A majority of the teaching workforce are White and female. In order to provide quality provision of care and education, Cushner, McClelland and Safford (1996) proposed six stages to become a bicultural teacher. This theory was originally related to American Indians. But these stages can be relevant to anyone who wishes to become bicultural. The six stages suggested are:

1. learning stereotypes and prejudices

2. confronting our prejudices

3. redefining our perceptions

4. opening ourselves to new experiences

5. adjusting and reshaping our identities

6. transformation as bicultural teachers.

It is important to acknowledge that there is no stipulated time for a teacher to go through the six stages of transformation to become a bicultural teacher. This can be challenging for teachers to relate to their own stereotypes and prejudices as they might have restricted opportunities and experience to realise this. Some people may take a shorter or longer time than others to progress from one stage to another. After going through these six stages, they might find themselves at the first stage again when they identify another of their stereotypes and/or prejudices.

## Iceberg concept of culture

Culture is compared to a big iceberg by Hall (1976), an anthropologist (see Figure 3.1). He suggests that the aspects of other cultures that are visible and familiar are like a tip of an iceberg and a large portion of culture is hidden beneath water. The tip of the iceberg relates to the explicit and concrete aspects of culture that are visible, and the largest part of the iceberg that is invisible relates to the beliefs and values and thought patterns which influence behaviour and are difficult to absorb. From an early childhood perspective, it is beneficial not only to be aware of different ways of greeting (verbally and gestures), but also to understand the rationale behind them. A practitioner could encourage a relationship with elders (extended family members) related to the child by involving parents and/or grandparents by inviting them into the setting to discuss celebrations, traditions, beliefs, etc. with the children.

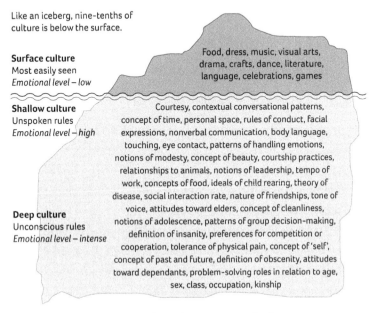

*Figure 3.1: The iceberg concept of culture*

Culture is a complicated phenomenon with several layers. Knowledge around culture is often perceived to relate to food, dress, language festivals, etc. and can be superficial. These symbols would differ from one family to another and would be easily identifiable. The signs and symbols found superficially are concrete and explicit. When these symbols are exhibited, they are often considered as the main ways of relating to other cultures. For example, practitioners in childcare settings may display a poster on different festivals; however, there might be very little awareness about the context and background about the festivals. Underneath the top layer, a lack of knowledge and understanding has been expressed by practitioners, especially with regard to the implicit and subconscious assumptions about the beliefs, norms and attitudes of a culture. A larger chunk of the culture is abstract and implicit. It will be difficult for a person who does not belong to a culture to identify with certain customs and understand the values and beliefs of another culture from outside.

It is also important to acknowledge that cultures are not homogenous; they are dynamic, and the majority culture influences the minority culture and vice versa. This is the reason why there are differences in the cultures of individuals from different generations living in different countries.

## CONCEPTS AROUND CULTURE AND EDUCATION

Multicultural education is an idea, an approach to school reform, and a movement for equity, social justice and democracy (Banks and Ambrosio, 2020). The National Association for Multicultural Education states: 'Multicultural education is a philosophical concept built on the ideals of freedom, justice, equality, equity and human dignity' (NAME, 2020). It recognises the role schools can play in developing the attitudes and values necessary for a democratic society. It values cultural differences and affirms the pluralism that students, their communities and teachers reflect. It challenges all forms of discrimination in schools and society through the promotion of democratic principles of social justice. Multicultural education is a process that permeates all aspects of school practices, policies and organisation as a means to ensure the highest levels of academic achievement for all students. It helps students develop a positive self-concept by providing knowledge about the histories, cultures and contributions of diverse groups.

Banks' (2015) *Dimensions of Multicultural Education* is used widely by school districts to conceptualise and develop courses, programmes and projects in multicultural education. The five dimensions are: (1) content integration; (2) the knowledge construction process; (3) prejudice reduction; (4) an equity pedagogy; and (5) an empowering school culture and social structure. Although each dimension is conceptually distinct, in practice they overlap and are interrelated.

An anti-bias curriculum is an approach to early childhood education that sets forth values-based principles and methodology in support of *respecting and embracing differences and acting against bias and unfairness.* Anti-bias teaching requires critical thinking and problem solving by both children and adults. The overarching goal is creating a climate of positive self and group identity development, through which every child will achieve her or his fullest potential.

## The four core goals of anti-bias education

- **Goal 1:** Each child will demonstrate self-awareness, confidence, family pride and positive social identities.

- **Goal 2:** Each child will express comfort and joy with human diversity; accurate language for human differences; and deep, caring human connections.

- **Goal 3:** Each child will increasingly recognise unfairness, have language to describe unfairness, and understand that unfairness hurts.

- **Goal 4:** Each child will demonstrate empowerment and the skills to act, with others or alone, against prejudice and/or discriminatory actions.

Ladson-Billings' (1994) research shows that five areas matter a great deal in the education of a multicultural population: teachers' beliefs about students, curriculum content and materials, instructional approaches, educational settings, and teacher education. One other area – whether the race and ethnicity of teachers affects student learning – remains unclear.

## Culturally relevant pedagogy

Ladson-Billings (1994) proposed culturally relevant teaching that helps teachers to use a 'pedagogy that empowers students intellectually, socially, emotionally, and politically by using cultural referents to impart knowledge, skills, and attitudes' (pp.17–18). She believes that culturally relevant pedagogy will empower children to achieve academically, gain cultural competence, and understand and critique the social order. Further, culturally relevant pedagogy is rooted in the belief that learning is a socially mediated process explicitly connected to students' cultural and linguistic experiences (Groulx and Silva, 2010).

It is important that teachers and practitioners working with young children must believe that everyone succeeds irrespective of the diversity of their backgrounds and individual differences. Paris (2012) proposed culturally sustaining pedagogy that 'seeks to perpetuate and foster – to sustain – linguistic, literate, and cultural pluralism as part of the democratic project of schooling' (p.95). This will ensure the diverse cultures will remain alive and are passed on to future generations.

Culturally relevant pedagogy influenced curricula in several countries, thereby encouraging early childhood settings to embed diverse cultural and linguistic experiences into daily routines and activities, such as introducing foreign languages, celebrations and festivals from different religions and cultures, using culturally relevant resources, etc.

Cultural pluralism in the current context refers to being aware of different cultures and valuing them to ensure everyone, irrespective of their background, is encouraged to keep their unique identity and be accepted by mainstream society. This will enable individuals belonging to minority ethnic groups to be respected, and it is understood as smaller diverse groups being accepted by the majority groups and still maintaining their unique cultural identity. Assimilation, on the other hand, demonstrates the value of diverse beliefs and enables the integration of all groups in the community.

Peter Adler (1974) referred to three basic pluralist principles. They are: (1) every culture has its own internal coherence, integrity and logic; (2) no culture is inherently better or worse than another; and (3) all persons are to some extent culturally bound.

Early childhood settings and schools must promote retaining the original culture of children and families from diverse backgrounds and not merely tolerating them. Tiedt and Tiedt (1990) suggest that teachers/practitioners should work together to understand cultures and empower one another. Pluralist educational experiences enable people to sustain cultures, rather than tolerating them or melting them down (Banks, 1988; Pizzillo, 1983). Pluralist teachers empower their students by constructing meaning together and thereby create a positive environment (Tiedt and Tiedt, 1990).

Gay and Kirkland (2003) recommend that teachers acknowledge the identities of children related to their race, culture and languages spoken, and indicate that what they are encouraged to bring with them into the classroom might influence them to feel discriminated against or privileged. Second, the teacher must engage in critical reflective practice to scrutinise his/her own ideological stance towards diversity. Without critical reflection, they might continue to justify their actions resulting in discrimination and thus they might harm the holistic development of children (Gay and Kirkland, 2003).

Hilliard (2006) recommends schools should abandon labels such as 'at risk' and 'disadvantaged' for diverse students and instead adopt the idea that all children have strengths that have to be identified. The cultural capital from a wide range of diverse homes will enrich the settings.

## LEGISLATION, POLICIES AND INITIATIVES

There are policies, legislation and initiatives put forward by influential global organisations, such as the United Nations, and by governments, at national and local levels. All early childhood settings must implement these policies and legislation and provide opportunities for children to access their rights.

The United Nations Convention on the Rights of the Child (UNCRC) is a political treaty that has been ratified by all countries apart from the United States. UNCRC has granted all children a comprehensive set of rights that has been signed and ratified by the UK government and came into force in 1992. Some of the articles that relate to culture include:

- ▶ Article 2: The Convention applies to every child without discrimination, whatever their ethnicity, gender, religion, language, abilities or any other status, whatever they think or say, whatever their family background.

- ▶ Article 8 (protection and preservation of identity): Every child has the right to an identity. Governments must respect and protect that right, and prevent the child's name, nationality or family relationships from being changed unlawfully.

- ▶ Article 14 (freedom of thought, belief and religion): Every child has the right to think and believe what they choose and also to practise their religion, as long as they are not stopping other people from enjoying their rights. Governments must respect the rights and responsibilities of parents to guide their child as they grow up.

- ▶ Article 30 (children from minority or indigenous groups): Every child has the right to learn and use the language, customs and religion of their family, whether or not these are shared by the majority of the people in the country where they live.

▶ Article 31 (leisure, play and culture): Every child has the right to relax, play and take part in a wide range of cultural and artistic activities.

## The national level

At a national level, there is legislation and guidance that will impact on children. This includes the following.

### EQUALITY ACT 2010

The Equality Act 2010 came into force in October 2010 and has replaced all previous legislation that protected the rights of individuals to be protected from unfair treatment and promote a fair and equal society. This law protects people with a 'protected characteristic' who should not be discriminated against. The protected characteristics include age, disability, gender reassessment, marriage and civil partnership, pregnancy and maternity, race, religion or belief, sex and sexual orientation.

This legislation recommends all childcare settings review policies and procedures related to rights and equal opportunities regularly and implement them in practice.

This legislation will have to be considered during the process of admission, when planning activities and when providing access to resources to promote optimum learning and development of children in childcare settings and schools.

### EARLY YEARS FOUNDATION STAGE (EYFS)

At national level, all early childhood settings are expected to implement the EYFS to ensure that their provision meets the learning and development needs of all children.

The EYFS is statutory, complying with the welfare regulations, as required by section 40 of the Childcare Act 2006. One of the key purpose and aims of the EYFS statutory framework is:

> All children, irrespective of ethnicity, culture or religion, home language, family background, learning difficulties or disabilities, gender or ability have the opportunity to experience a challenging and enjoyable programme of learning and development.

The EYFS comprises four themes. Under the theme 'Unique child', the second principle refers to inclusive practice. One of the commitments is titled 'Equality and diversity'. Two of the statements under Theme 1.2 Equality and Diversity are relevant specifically to all children irrespective of their culture.

The EYFS states in principle 1.2 'A unique child: Inclusive practice': 'All children are entitled to enjoy a full life in conditions which will help them take part in society and develop as an individual, with their own cultural and spiritual beliefs', and 'Practitioners [must] ensure that their own knowledge about different cultural groups is up-to-date and consider their own attitudes to people who are different from themselves.'

### NATIONAL CURRICULUM

The National Curriculum (1999) expects all schools to implement the National Curriculum Inclusion Statement.

DfE (2014a) refers to the National Curriculum Statutory Inclusion Statement, which asserts:

> Schools have a responsibility to provide a broad and balanced curriculum for all pupils. The National Curriculum is the starting point for planning a school curriculum that meets the specific needs of individuals and groups of pupils.

The Inclusion Statement sets out three principles that are essential to developing a more inclusive curriculum:

- setting suitable learning challenges

- responding to pupils' diverse learning needs
- overcoming potential barriers to learning and assessment for individuals and groups of pupils.

## RESEARCH

A wide range of research has been done on this topic in different countries around the world. Key research themes include: key role of practitioner/teacher to include all children and parents; engaging families; preparedness and confidence of teachers to teach children from diverse families; experiences (positive and negative) of children from migrant families in early childhood settings; and perceptions of staff relating to migrant children and their abilities.

Teacher training institutions are still very traditional in their approach to preparing teachers for working in classrooms, and often ignore children from other cultures, instead focusing on the students that they are comfortable dealing with, rather than the marginalised (Porfilio and Malott, 2011).

Lynch and Hanson (1998) believe that practitioners may find it difficult to gain an understanding of every minority culture and languages that may be different to the dominant language in that culture. They suggest that settings can acquire insights into relevant local and regional cultures by encouraging families to provide support through sharing resources, and helping to interpret languages and cultures. They indicate that it is important to be aware of one's own values and beliefs, as well as those of parents, children and families. Further, it is also important to be aware of any differences in values related to gender, social and economic circumstances, education and the number of years they have lived in the community.

Winterbottom (2013) explored the perception of Japanese mothers living in Florida, who had mixed opinions regarding

American preschools and teachers; they felt frustrated and highlighted their concerns that were then classified into three categories: language barriers, cultural issues, and structural support (limited state, school and teacher support) in building relationships with teachers (relating to communication with preschool teachers). They referred to the inadequate communication skills of teachers to support the immigrant parents, losing their Japanese cultural heritage, as well as lack of opportunities to communicate about their child's progress and to develop relationships with the teachers.

Hamilton (2013) studied a local authority in North East Wales with little experience of cultural and linguistic diversity to identify if migrant children have access to education and social opportunities, and if they are able to make successful transitions to new school environments. Practitioners need to be proactive and reflective of their own cultural and linguistic positioning, value base and pedagogy. As the local authority had little experience of catering for cultural and linguistic diversity, practitioners were challenged by the lack of training, written guidance and suitable teaching resources.

Van Laere and Vandenbroeck (2017) studied the multiple meanings that parents and preschool staff working with young children between two-and-a-half and four years old attributed to early learning in preschool. It was interesting to realise that parents and preschool staff had similar, although contrasting, meanings related to early learning. Parents, particularly of migrant children, had an omnipresent fear of exclusion in early learning. They considered preschool staff as gatekeepers to inclusion (i.e. through language support), although the teachers did not explicitly recognise this role. Instead, they referred to children from migrant backgrounds as being 'language poor' or 'having language delay' and believed that these children were not motivated or interested in early learning. This indicates that preschool staff perceive that dual-language learners are challenging and the child or the parent are identified as the problem, rather than considering how these children add value to the school environment or that they are responsible for children's learning. The study recommended that preschool staff constantly review their conceptualisations of early learning, so that it can benefit all children, including migrant children.

Preschoolers need repeated exposure to the anti-bias curriculum for it to be effective. Activities that focus on building self-awareness and pride based on personal traits and background are part of the curriculum. These activities might focus on what makes each child unique, such as a self-portrait that highlights features or a poster that shows each child's traits and interests.

Flood (2018) reported on the research conducted by the Centre for Literacy in Primary Education (CLPE) (2019) investigating the number of children's books that had representation of BAME characters. They surveyed children's books published in the UK. The results indicated that only a quarter of books related to diversity, and just 4 per cent of the characters were from a BAME background and 1 per cent were main characters. She quotes Nikesh Shukla, an author who believes:

> When you're figuring out the world, being able to see yourself in books, as well as people who don't look like you, is really important. It means you see your story as valid, and it can contribute to who you imagine yourself to be – and a kid should be able to imagine themselves as anyone in the world. These mirrors are so important.

### Reflection point

Audit the story books in your setting and identify:

- How many books cover diversity and what issues do they include?

- How many story books feature BAME children as the main characters?

- What is the context of the main characters – positive or sad?

- How frequently are these books read to the children?

The National Association for the Education of Young Children (NAEYC) (n.d.) warns of a 'tourist curriculum', where references are made to different cultures occasionally without integrating into everyday routines.

The 'tourist approach' relates to how culture is embedded into the curriculum, but it provides a restricted perspective, for example about a celebration that has been generalised and is superficial due to brief exposure to the event. Some practitioners may be biased towards children from diverse backgrounds. However, the bias can be due to conscious, subconscious and unconscious bias. Many teachers currently in the classroom report that they feel inadequate to teach due to inadequate training and awareness of appropriate strategies related to multicultural or anti-bias curriculum (Au and Blake, 2003; Ukpokodu, 2004). Van Hook (2002) believes that teacher educators and teachers may find it difficult to teach children from diverse backgrounds, as they experience fear, uncertainty and discomfort that may become barriers due to their presumptions about children from diverse families.

Ramsey (1982) described some potential problems with a multicultural curriculum. First, it frequently focuses on other countries (e.g. China or Mexico) rather than learning about, for example, the cultural diversity of Chinese Americans or Mexican Americans. Second, multicultural curricula may be standardised, rather than taking into account the background and experiences of a unique group of children. Third, teachers may assume that children only need a multicultural curriculum if there is diversity in the classroom. Thus, a teacher in an all-White classroom might feel that a multicultural approach is not needed. The diversity within the same culture may be overlooked. The relevance of these findings might apply in different countries.

The most serious disadvantage of multicultural approaches is slipping in to a 'tourist curriculum' (Derman-Sparks and the ABC Task Force, 1989) when a teacher relates to different cultures through celebrations, special foods, displays of traditional clothes and decorations without much discussion. The superficial knowledge and understanding related to multicultural activities in the classroom might become a tokenistic way of bringing in multiculturalism in the classroom. The anti-bias approach is a way to challenge prejudice, stereotyping and bias. According to Derman-Sparks and the ABC Task Force (1989), the anti-bias curriculum focuses on the multicultural curriculum and avoids the tourist approach.

Teacher educators and students understand that there is no single 'right' way to work with all children, and no 'recipe' or 'guide map'. 'There is no single formula for preparing the next generation of teachers to work with the variety of cultures that they may come in to contact with during their career' (Meece and Wingate, 2010, p.42).

Vandenbroeck (2011) highlighted that, for many migrant children, attending an early childhood setting might be their first experience of the new society, and the responses of practitioners will reflect society's attitudes towards them.

Picchio and Mayer (2019) explored the experience of young children, aged 18–36 months and 36–48 months, from migrant families attending an early childhood education and care (ECEC) service for the first time. They studied how the children adapted to the socially, culturally and linguistically different context from their home. Most children were distressed and faced a difficult transition. They explained it by suggesting that children experienced double transition: meeting unfamiliar adults and peers; and meeting expectations related to different behaviours, rules, habits and different language. Their findings reported that children's experiences became positive through active participation in care and play activities with teachers and peers. They recommended that 'it is essential to build an educational context that enhances their identity, in which cultural diversity is immediately recognized and made visible to all children and their families' (p.294).

Lee (2019) discusses her challenges of being a minority parent experiencing racial discrimination in the American education system. Despite being well educated and able to express fluently, she felt that the problem is more than cultural insensitivity and misunderstanding. She recommends that schools encourage practitioners to acknowledge and confront racism in the school. She believes that 'Language isn't the sole barrier to minority parents' participation; schools should also make efforts to help parents understand local policies, school rules, and expectations for student behavior and performance' (p.32). She also highlights the role of teacher educators 'to push the pre-service and in-service teachers beyond their comfort zone as they acknowledge their racial identity as a social construction molded by history and colored by personal experiences' (p.33).

The primary school classrooms have seen a significant shift in the diversity of children. Ainscow *et al.* (2016) assert that '[the] most apparently homogenous classroom is in fact diverse simply because no two children are identical in educational terms. The most overt markers of difference, such as ethnicity or social class, are simply indicators of the underlying diversity that characterises schools and classrooms' (p.3).

## ACTIVITY: CELEBRATIONS

This is a circle time activity with children and their parents. Ask the children to narrate how they celebrate Christmas, with additional information provided by their parent/s. Prepare some pointers such as:

- Do you celebrate Christmas?

- How do you celebrate it?

- What are the traditions related to this celebration? Describe your routine – is it different to your normal day?

- Discuss the similarities and differences in how all children and families celebrate different occasions. What are the similarities and differences and the reasons for the same?

## AUDIT OF MULTICULTURAL RESOURCES AND EXPERIENCES IN AN EARLY CHILDHOOD SETTING

- What multicultural resources are available in your setting? Make a list.

- What is the relevance of these resources in the current context? Do they reinforce or challenge stereotypes?

- Are these resources accessible by children?

- How often are they used?

- Are children allowed to bring in artefacts or things that they can identify with or that represent their identity?

- How are parents engaged in the setting, especially to share their perspectives and experiences of culture?

- Are practitioners/teachers encouraged to share their own experiences and perspectives of different celebrations?

- How often does the setting benefit from making links with key people and visiting multicultural places – places of worship and community centres related to different religions and countries located in the community?

Table 3.1 shows the challenges related to culture experienced by children, practitioners and settings and the government at different levels in multicultural society. What are the implications of providing quality provision for children, families and practitioners and government?

**Table 3.1: Cultural challenges**

| Children and families | Practitioners/ teachers in settings | Government |
|---|---|---|
| Self-esteem and identity | Preparedness to teach | Policies |
| Achievement | Priorities for training teachers/ practitioners | Education and training provision |
| Support provided to meet the needs of the child | Funding for provision | Influence of international policies |
| Being accepted | Choice of appropriate resources | Influence of shifts in culture |
| Access to schools and services | Ethos of schools and settings and attitudes to diversity | Curriculum for teacher trainees and young children |

## DEBATES AND CONTROVERSIES

- Culture is not homogenous. Some children's cultures can be overlooked as they can be presumed to be 'normal' as everyone else. Differences can be invisible.

- How aware are early childhood settings and schools of meeting the needs of children from different cultural backgrounds and how feasible is it for them to meet those needs?

- Do teachers and practitioners have the ability to communicate with children and families from bi/multicultural families?

- Are teachers and practitioners well prepared to teach children from diverse backgrounds?

- Consider the attitudes of teachers and practitioners towards children and families from different cultures and who speak English as an additional language.

- Is cultural awareness and sensitivity relevant in only multicultural and diverse settings? What about settings with predominantly a monocultural or White population?

- Is diversity considered an opportunity or a threat? What are the key drivers to bring shifts in understanding of diversity?

- Instead of assuming that absence of participation is an indication of parents not being concerned about their children, practitioners must understand the barriers that hinder some parents from participating in their child's education.

- Parents whose voices are rarely heard at school explain how the diverse contexts of their lives create tensions that interfere with positive home/school relations. For them, their own school experiences, economic and time constraints, and linguistic and cultural practices have produced a body of knowledge about school settings that frequently goes unacknowledged.

- The right age to introduce diversity and difference to young children has been disputed by several experts (Connolly 2002).

## Some key points from the chapter

×   Context of diversity – a multicultural and diverse population has become a global trend especially in the developed and rich countries. Meeting the needs of children from diverse families has been gaining the attention of stakeholders from different levels, from the grassroots level to policy makers at the government level, and is considered to be a challenge in several countries around the world.

×   Ignoring or denying differences is not sustainable and ethical in the current educational context. Neither is tokenism and the tourist curriculum.

×   Debates on diversity are increasingly relevant in the contemporary society due to an influx of migrants from a large number of developing and underdeveloped countries into different rich and developed countries for safety and career and economic progression.

×   Inclusive schools must be committed to be open and flexible towards diverse identities and perspectives. Approaches and ideologies are needed that provide opportunities to all children to achieve the best of their potential through an appropriate curriculum, resources and activities reinforcing learning and development.

×   Research and literature have made references to the tourist curriculum and emphasised the importance of preparing the practitioners to meet the unique needs of children from diverse backgrounds. This is believed to be a key issue due to the influx of migrants in many developed countries.

# 4

# English as an Additional Language (EAL)

This chapter will focus on:

- concepts and terminology of EAL

- theories and perspectives of learning languages

- curriculum and learning

- dilemmas and controversies related to languages.

## INTRODUCTION

The UK population has been becoming more diverse, as a result of migration from different countries and ethnic minority groups speaking English as an additional language with variable proficiencies in English. These children might be originally from Asian, African, South American or European countries. People who speak English as an additional language are not a homogenous group, due to their varied proficiencies and ability to speak the language, length of their stay in the country and status – migrants and refugees may be confident, educated and skilled, uneducated and unskilled, under-confident, apprehensive or discriminated against. People from the same country may have different ethnic, religious, political or social class backgrounds and may speak more than one or two languages other than English.

Some children speak only one language (when their mother tongue, home language and first language are all the same). Others may be bi- or multilingual, as a result of being exposed to different languages (as their mother tongue can be different to their home language and or first language) at home, in the neighbourhood, early childhood settings and schools, and with their peer group, enabling them to gain proficiencies in one or more of these languages to speak, read and/or write.

Some European countries, such as England, Spain, Portugal and France, and colonised countries in Asia, Africa and South America, have been largely influential in spreading English, Spanish, Portuguese and French around the world.

Globally, multilingualism is the norm and monolingualism the exception. For example, bilingualism or multilingualism is officially prevalent in countries such as Belgium (Lijphart, 1981), with the Dutch-speaking Flemish in the north and French-speaking Walloons in the south; Canada, which has French and English as official languages; and Switzerland, where four national languages, French, German, Italian and Romansch, are recognised from four cantons or territories (Billigmeier, 2016; Klode, 1988). India has Hindi as an official language and English is used for official purposes to communicate between the central government and the state governments, and 22 other languages are recognised as scheduled languages in Article 34 of the Indian constitution.[1]

England's population has evolved over centuries and the diversity of children's backgrounds is reflected in schools. Over 30 per cent of pupils are from an ethnic minority background (DfE, 2019) and almost one in six pupils speaks English as an Additional Language (EAL) (Bell Foundation, 2017).

In predominantly monolingual countries, bilingualism and

---

1 www.india.gov.in/my-government/constitution-india/constitution-india-full-text

multilingualism may be perceived to be a challenge due to restricted opportunities to be exposed to different languages. However, there are advantages of being bi- or multilingual for individuals with respect to cognitive development, ageing complications, linguistic awareness, communicative competence and academic or educational performance, as well as sociocultural and economic benefits for multilingual societies related to the economy, culture, education, security and health (Chibaka, 2018).

## CONCEPTS AND TERMINOLOGY

Monolingualism, bilingualism and multilingualism are terms that refer to the abilities of individuals to speak one, two or more than two languages. The Department for Education (DfE, 2013c, p.7) defines 'first language' as 'The language to which a child was initially exposed to during early development and continues to be exposed in the home or in the community'.

Some terms such as mother tongue, home language and first language are used loosely. A child is exposed to these languages at home as different adults (parent/s, nanny, staff in the childcare setting) and peers in the neighbourhood speak with them.

The term 'mother language', or 'mother tongue', is the language spoken from earliest childhood. Dixon (2018) describes 'home language' as 'the first language we learn to speak and is generally the language of our parents and community', and notes that 'Sometimes we can have multiple home languages'.

There are several terms and concepts used in different countries where English is the major language spoken, such as the UK, USA, Australia, Canada and New Zealand. There are different terms used in these countries to refer to someone who speaks English as a second, third or fourth language or who is learning to speak English outside their home.

- ELL – English Language Learner is a term used in the

USA and Canada to describe a person who is learning the English language in addition to his or her native language or any other languages they may speak.

- ESL – English as a Second Language. ESL is used in the United States, an English-speaking nation. ESL students learn English as a Second Language in a country where English is the predominant language.

- EAL – English as an Additional Language is used in the UK.

- Balanced multilingualism – a pedagogical approach that allows teachers to be open to other languages and cultures. This enables teachers to relate to different languages and cultures.

- Additive bilingualism is the 'process of developing bilingual and bicultural skills' in children who, 'with no fear of ethnic/linguistic erosion, can add one or more foreign languages to their accumulating skills, and profit immensely from the experience, cognitively, socially and even economically' (Lambert, 1983, pp.99–100).

- Subtractive bilingualism refers to the first language of the child being gradually replaced when a second language is learnt, resulting in the loss of mother tongue or first language. Until the age of about 12, a person's language skills are relatively vulnerable to change.

- Code switching relates to bilinguals or multilinguals, who are able to speak more than one language in one conversation or sometimes able to talk in different languages with different people. Code switching enables the child to develop the ability to be flexible to use different languages and adapt to people who speak different languages and contexts. For example, a three-year-old child with two parents speaking different languages is able to switch between both the languages while talking to both parents. This child may speak in a different language with his or her babysitter who might speak in a third language. Further, the child may speak in a fourth language in the nursery or school if the majority language is different. A child whose parents speak two Indian languages (Hindi and Bengali) and who is taken care of by a Polish nanny, living in London, might speak all four languages – Hindi, Bengali, Polish and English. Code switching occurs when a speaker alternates between two or more languages, or language varieties, in the context of a single conversation.

- Crossing is a term for situations where people from various ethnic backgrounds borrow terminology and patterns from various languages, not considered to 'belong' to them, and insert them into their conversation in order to socialise. Taylor (2013) refers to 'crossing as a key feature of multi-ethnic societies, and is not restricted to young people alone, but has also been identified as a working-class phenomenon as well' (p.2). While speaking different languages with other people, the child might be crossing between more than one language in a single conversation. Sometimes, it may not be possible to mix words and phrases from the majority language while talking in a mother tongue, which may be a minority language. For example, in countries such as India which was one of the British colonies, several English words such as bus, train, cycle and phone are commonly used by the general population including those who are not literate in English. Further, there are several commonly used words in English that have been borrowed from other languages.

- Translanguaging is a concept that allows children an

opportunity to alternate between their first and second languages. It is usually allowed in early childhood settings where young children can insert some words from their mother tongue to communicate in formal settings. However, some primary schools encourage translanguaging to promote deeper and fuller understanding and enable the children to gain an understanding of concepts in a better manner.

From personal experience, it is common for an individual to use two to three languages in one conversation when code switching as well as translanguaging. This is not only observed in the UK but also in India. If the practitioner or teacher is not familiar with the EAL child's mother tongue or first language and forms of communication using words from different languages, it might become a barrier to communicate with adults and children.

## STATISTICS

There has been a steady increase in EAL children since 2006. The DfE (2018) reported that 21.2 per cent of children spoke English as an additional language in primary schools and 16.6 per cent in secondary schools.

These figures do not mean that there is lack of proficiency in English language in all these children. A child is 'exposed to more than one language (which may include English) during early development the language other than English should be recorded irrespective of the child's proficiency in English' (DfE, 2015, p.8). Similarly, the census figures do not distinguish between children born outside the UK whose first language is not English and second-generation children born in the UK who are either bilingual or whose first language is not English (see also Strand, 2007; Strand and Demie, 2006).

Arnot and colleagues (2014, p.12) believe that the category of

EAL student is characterised as a 'pupil whose first language is known or believed to be other than English'. For almost all EAL learners, this means that if they are an EAL learner when they start school at three to five years old, they will be an EAL learner throughout their education and their life. This can be challenged as there are differences in proficiencies in different languages in children who are new arrivals compared to those who are fully fluent due to their domicile in the country for a few generations.

Some EAL children may learn English in the first few months of entering an early childhood setting or later in mainstream education and achieve as well as their English-speaking peers. However, this can depend on the age at which the child enters the UK. If a child enters at a later age, the child might need a lot more support. Demie (2013) reported that it takes about five to seven years to acquire academic English proficiency, so it is beneficial if a child learns a second or third language at a very early age.

Pupils who have English as an additional language are not a homogenous group. The proficiency of their English language will depend on their exposure to the language. For example, a newly arrived asylum seeker may have limited English skills compared to another child whose family has been settled in the UK for a few generations. However, some new immigrants can have good understanding of the language, especially reading and writing, but may struggle to speak fluently or understand other pupils speaking English as their mother tongue or first language due to their accents and lack of familiarity with slang and colloquialisms. For example, idioms such as 'it is raining cats and dogs' might not make much sense. Pronunciation of certain names and words where some letters may remain silent may be a challenge to immigrants (even with English proficiency as a result of learning from non-native speakers). There are issues around spoken language relating to regional accents and lack of awareness and understanding of local slang and dialects. The ability of children to speak English might have an impact on how the EAL child might be included by their peers in different activities that will influence their holistic development and achievement. Further, teachers might stereotype EAL children and might have low expectations in relation to their proficiencies in English and academic attainment (Evans *et al.* 2016).

## THEORIES

Theories related to learning languages such as balloon theory and iceberg theory discussed below provide different perspectives on being bilingual or monolingual in an early childhood setting.

In balloon theory, it is imagined that bilingual people have two balloons representing the two languages inside the head. It is believed that when a child learns a second language, the first language balloon shrinks in size or vice versa. This suggests that children cannot learn two languages at the same time. Perhaps some preschools in the UK are influenced by this theory when they advise families not to speak to their child in their mother tongue, so that the child can learn English (their second language) faster. Cummins (1980) refers to this phenomenon as the Separate Underlying Model of Bilingualism. The model indicates that the two languages work independently of each other, and no transfer occurs.

Another perspective, iceberg theory, disagrees with this model, positing that children are able to transfer information from their first language to the second and vice versa. This is supported by the Common Underlying Proficiency Model of Bilingualism proposed by Cummins. The model is represented in the form of two icebergs. The concept is that the two languages are separated above the surface but underneath the surface they are fused. Lessons or skills learned in one language can be transferred to the other language. Being multilingual, my personal experiences indicate that several concepts learnt in my own mother tongue can be transferred into the second or third language, which may be the medium of the lessons taught in school. This can help the child to understand the concept better.

Stephen Krashen (1987) proposed five stages of second language acquisition.

## Stages of learning a second language

1. The silent period – This stage can last from several hours to about six months. The child might be quiet and might use their home language and gestures. Often the child will start with a silent period, possibly combined with gestures and some use of their home language. This child might be absorbing the new language by observing and becoming familiar with the new contexts. During this time, this child can be encouraged to use nonverbal responses when possible and continue to speak as much as possible.

2. Early production – This stage may last about six months, during which language learners typically acquire an understanding of up to 1,000 words. They may also learn to speak some words and begin forming short phrases, even though they may not be grammatically correct.

3. Speech emergence – By this stage, learners typically acquire a vocabulary of up to 3,000 words, and learn to communicate by putting the words in short phrases, sentences and questions. Again, they may not be grammatically correct, but this is an important stage during which learners gain greater comprehension and begin reading and writing in their second language.

4. Intermediate fluency – At this stage, which may last for a year or more after speech emergence, learners typically have a vocabulary of as many as 6,000 words.

They usually acquire the ability to communicate in writing and speech using more complex sentences. This crucial stage is also when learners begin actually thinking in their second language, which helps them gain more proficiency in speaking it.

5. Continued language development/advanced fluency – It takes most learners at least two years to reach this stage, and then up to ten years to achieve full mastery of the second language in all its complexities and nuances. Second language learners need ongoing opportunities to engage in discussions and express themselves in their new language, in order to maintain fluency in it.

## RESEARCH

This section will focus on research published on a range of issues, including conflicts between parents' aspirations and practitioners' expectations for children to learn the majority language, in addition to tensions around maintaining the mother tongue, impact of speaking and not speaking the mother tongue, impact of learning a second language, and impact on achievements and assessments.

Xiaoxia Li (1999) explored how parents balanced first language spoken at home and the majority language spoken outside the house from two perspectives: (1) parents' attitudes towards first and second languages (L1 and L2) and cultures (valuing the heritage and respecting the new); and (2) parent–child interactions – communication between family members ensuring the home language or mother tongue is maintained to bridge the generation gap, and promoting simultaneous use of both the languages at home. The study showed that parents' positive attitudes toward both languages and cultures and supportive interactions with their children at home are very important to the children's bilingual education and identity establishment in the new environment.

On the other hand, Jiangbo Hu, Jane Torr and Peter Whiteman (2014) explored educators' views on children's use of their mother tongue in early childhood settings, including the conflicts between the parental expectation and educator views on children's use of their mother tongue. Settings and practitioners reported that many Chinese parents expected their children to speak in English rather than their mother tongue in early childhood settings. This expectation did not support educators' beliefs about pedagogical practices that promoted children to speak in their mother tongue and respect their heritage. Parents believed that their children speaking English in the settings will enable them to be accepted by their peers. The educators developed different strategies to address the tension between their desire to achieve positive outcomes for children and their need to work in partnership with families.

## TEACHERS' CONFIDENCE TO TEACH EAL CHILDREN

Early childhood settings and schools have reported that teaching EAL children is challenging (Evans *et al.*, 2016). Annual Newly Qualified Teacher (NQT) surveys question NQTs on their confidence on a range of issues around teaching children from different backgrounds, including ethnic minorities or children who speak English as an additional language. Significant low confidence of NQTs to teach children from ethnic minorities has been reported consistently since 2003 when these questions were introduced. 'Despite the longer term increase in the proportion of positive responses to this question since 2008, this is one of the lowest rated aspects of teacher training for primary trainees' (NCTL, 2015, p.48).

Is it due to limited knowledge and understanding and/or lack of confidence due to inadequate references to diversity and inclusion in the teacher training curriculum and not prioritising issues related to ethnic minorities?

Are NQTs not confident teaching children from minority groups and those who speak EAL as a result of their stereotypes and prejudices? They could be presuming that the challenges of teaching these children are due to the children's poor abilities and skills, but it is important to be aware of the diverse nature of the abilities and skills of all children.

Table 4.1 shows the percentage of NQTs who responded 'Very good' or 'Good' to the question 'How good was your training in preparing you to teach pupils from all ethnic backgrounds?'

**Table 4.1: How NQTs rated their training in terms of diversity**

|  | Primary | | Secondary | |
|---|---|---|---|---|
|  | Very good | Good | Very good | Good |
| 2006 | 9 | 27 | 11 | 26 |
| 2008 | 9 | 29 | 11 | 30 |
| 2010 | 11 | 32 | 11 | 30 |
| 2012 | 16 | 38 | 18 | 34 |
| 2015 | 27 | 39 | 36 | 39 |

NQTs responded that their training was rated less positively for ensuring that their teaching meets the needs of pupils from all ethnic backgrounds and for those for whom English is an additional language at primary and secondary levels.

It is clear that there is an improvement from 2006 to 2015 in terms of how prepared NQTs feel to teach pupils from ethnic minorities and pupils with English as an additional language. This is important when we consider the number of migrant families seeking refuge in different countries for safety. If teachers are feeling inadequately prepared to teach children from ethnic minority families as well as those who speak English as an additional language, then these children might not be able to reach their full potential. This might not only impact on the child's holistic development, but also provide discrepancies in identifying their needs or special needs and assessment and progress or achievement.

## ASSESSMENT OF EAL CHILDREN

Should English-speaking children and non-English-speaking children be assessed in the same way? Is it fair for an EAL young child to be assessed in English, when they are not able to perform as well as they can? Are practitioners and teachers able to assess the child with EAL appropriately?

The Early Years Foundation Stage (EYFS) provides the following guidance for assessing children:

> 1.8 For children whose home language is not English, providers must take reasonable steps to provide opportunities for children to develop and use their home language in play and learning, supporting their language development at home. Providers must also ensure that children have sufficient opportunities to learn and reach a good standard in English language during the EYFS, ensuring children are ready to benefit from the opportunities available to them when they begin Year 1. When assessing communication, language and literacy skills, practitioners must assess children's skills in English. If a child does not have a strong grasp of English language, practitioners must explore the child's skills in the home language with parents and/or carers, to establish whether there is cause for concern about language delay. (DfE, 2012a, p.6)

> The EYFS profile assessment is underpinned by an understanding that language is central to our sense of identity and belonging to a community. The profile recognises and values linguistic diversity. (p.18)

The 3 aspects specific to the assessment of children for whom English is not their home language are: • development in their home language • development across areas of learning, assessed through their home language • development of English. Within the EYFS profile, the ELGs for communication and language, and for literacy, must be assessed in relation to the child's competency in English. The remaining ELGs may be assessed in the context of any language – including their home language and English. (Standards and Testing Agency, 2017, p.20)

Despite this guidance, there are challenges faced by practitioners and teachers to meet the needs of children and support them appropriately.

## THE NATIONAL CURRICULUM AND EAL CHILDREN

The DfE (2014a) refers to teachers' standards in *The National Curriculum in England: Key Stages 3 and 4 Framework Document.*

Teaching Standard 4.5 Teachers must also take account of the needs of pupils whose first language is not English. Monitoring of progress should take account of the pupil's age, length of time in this country, previous educational experience and ability in other languages.

Teaching Standard 4.6 The ability of pupils for whom English is an additional language to take part in the national curriculum may be in advance of their communication skills in English. Teachers should plan teaching opportunities to help pupils develop their English and should aim to provide the support pupils need to take part in all subjects. (p.8)

## EDUCATION INSPECTION FRAMEWORK OF OFSTED AND EAL

NALDIC, the national subject association for English as an additional language (2019), responding to the new Ofsted framework, stated that it 'make[s] explicit reference to EAL as either a discrete focus or a paradigm'. EAL must not be considered as a threat but an opportunity. Schools must ensure they are proud of the multilinguistic abilities of EAL pupils and should use them to help all children. However, there are limited references to EAL learners visible in the inspection framework.

Since 2016, all schools in England are expected to report on Proficiency in English for all their EAL learners over four years old. There is also a pupil tracking tool for teachers to monitor and record the progress of EAL learners, and ensure accurate records of language development are maintained.

## THE BELL FOUNDATION'S EAL ASSESSMENT FRAMEWORK FOR SCHOOLS

The Bell Foundation's EAL Assessment Framework for Schools (Version 1.1) is an assessment tool for assessing learners with English as an additional language. The Assessment Framework includes support strategies suitable for the EYFS, primary and secondary. EAL assessment is important not only for those who are new learners but all EAL/bilingual learners who have to develop their academic English to achieve according to their age. Appropriate assessment enables a teacher to identify a learner's abilities and potential to learn. On the other hand, inappropriate assessment can result in the child given an incorrect judgement of their needs and might have an impact on their development.

Practitioners and teachers must work alongside the families of children with EAL to ensure the child is not judged wrongly based on their inability to respond in English. Practitioners can collaborate with parents to assess the child in their home language by observing the child for a period of time. The child can then be assessed using a wide range of assessments such as formative assessments, general observations, a Learning Journey, language assessments and possible video recording of the child at home (with translation by the parents) and checked against Development Matters statements (or Foundation Stage Profile – depending on the age of the child). Assessments done with parents in their mother tongue will enable the assessor to also see how the child responds/understands in their home language. When assessing children, practitioners must ensure the child is healthy to rule out any medical/health issues (such as hearing loss) and should monitor and review the child's learning regularly so that SEN can be identified at an early stage.

## HOW TO IDENTIFY AND SUPPORT EAL LEARNERS WITH SPECIAL EDUCATIONAL NEEDS

Practitioners should not assume that a child who is unable to speak English may have a learning problem or be less intelligent. It is important to identify children who may need additional support due to a specific learning need. Early intervention might ensure every child develops to the best of his or her potential. Further, despite the parents' awareness of relevant and specific information about the child's needs, they might consider the experts to be superior because of their professional status and expertise.

Perceptions of superiority attached to White people and proficiency in English language may result in diverse families being valued less than their White peers and so their family involvement may be inadequate (Kalyanpur, 1998; Leonardo, 2002). Children from diverse families may face discrimination that results in their poor educational experiences and low achievement; these negative experiences can lead to feeling unsafe, unwelcome and unsuccessful in school (Fazel, 2015; Goff *et al.,* 2014). The partnership between settings and culturally and linguistically diverse families may not be easy due to the barriers related to low value, poor status and lack of respect for the families (Burke, 2017).

Hutchinson (2018) examined the support provided for the educational outcomes of EAL children and reported the following findings. Compared to other countries, England's system for developing support for EAL pupils through specialist roles is insufficient. English-speaking areas, such as New York State, Minnesota, Alberta, New South Wales and New Zealand, promote far more extensive EAL policies. As a result of funds no longer being ringfenced for EAL pupils, and overall budgetary pressures, the supply of EAL expertise in schools has declined significantly. There is a noticeable absence of any mechanism which generates specialist expertise on EAL education, with England lacking national oversight or provision of professional qualifications, staff development and specialist roles for teachers and staff working with EAL children.

## CONTROVERSIES AND DILEMMAS

### Reflection points

What is the best age to introduce a second language? Is it best to introduce one language at a time? When an EAL child starts nursery at a young age, is the child encouraged to speak in English and advised not to speak in their mother tongue?

Is a practitioner or teacher able to relate to multiple minority languages to support EAL children and their families?

Young children can learn a second language for social communication from peers at school (Chamot and O'Malley, 1994). Bach (2017) reported that exposure to a foreign language stimulates infants' learning and that learning another language happens almost effortlessly. Young children can learn a second language to communicate with peers and for academic purposes.

Gill (2013) presented research exploring how practitioners and parents perceived the mother tongue of young children and how this was implemented in early years settings. Some of the key findings included:

- Parents believed that it is important for the child to maintain the home language. Many immigrant parents preferred the school to take responsibility for second language acquisition and the home for first language maintenance. Parents believed in a hierarchy in the value of languages, with a higher status given to European languages like French, German, Spanish and Italian compared to Arabic, Chinese, Hindi, Urdu, Punjabi, Swahili, etc. This might result in children giving a low value to non-European languages and not being given many opportunities to learn their mother tongue and considering their own mother tongue to be not important.

- Practitioners on the other hand felt that a bilingual or multilingual environment in their classroom would lead to language confusion and were worried about the acquisition of second language spoken and taught at school rather than the loss of the mother tongue.

- Schools and settings may have different priorities, and supporting EAL children may not rank highly due to inadequate availability of appropriate resources and restricted funding.

## Maintaining the mother tongue

Some parents believe that the use of a mother tongue may delay the acquisition of language and thus impede the child's involvement, interaction and inclusion with the peer group. The practitioner might advise the parents not to use their mother tongue at home and also to use English, so that the child does not get confused. This results in the loss of the child's own language/mother tongue and the child not being able to communicate with the elderly in the family or lose their cultural identity. This might also have an impact on the relationships between the child and the elderly family members, especially grandparents.

## Introduction of second languages at school

There are several countries around the world that have introduced more than one language when the child starts school. Seventy per cent of the world's population are bilingual. It is normal for children to be introduced and/or exposed to more than one or two languages when they attend an early childhood setting. Being exposed to more than one language will provide an opportunity to the child to relate to different structures and formats (reading, writing), awareness of different cultures and being able to appreciate and respect differences.

## Valuing diverse languages

There is positive research evidence emphasising the impact of being bi- or multilingual. Some diverse communities consider learning different languages to be an opportunity, while predominantly English-speaking communities may find it a threat.

Is it pertinent in diverse communities where it is considered to be an opportunity to learn different languages? What about schools with children who are predominantly English speaking – is introducing a second language considered to be a threat?

## Reflection point

Why are there still some countries that are predominantly monolingual? Some young people may consider themselves to be monolingual, despite learning other European languages in their secondary school. Is it due to their lack of confidence in the languages learnt or the relevance of the proficiency in the language to enable them to speak with confidence, or the ways in which the languages were taught?

## LEGISLATION, POLICIES AND INITIATIVES PROMOTING MINORITY LANGUAGES

The rights of the child who has English as an additional language and their family to relate to their own mother tongue, first language or home language have been highlighted in several international and national policies, legislation and curricula.

- ▶ UNCRC Article 30: In those States in which ethnic, religious or linguistic minorities or persons of indigenous origin exist, a child belonging to such a minority or who is indigenous shall not be denied the right, in community with other members of his or her group, to enjoy his or her own culture, to profess and practise his or her own religion, or to use his or her own language.

Cummins (2005) reminds us that the bilingual learner's pre-existing knowledge for English language is encoded *in their home language*. Therefore we should *explicitly* teach in a way that fosters transfer of concepts and skills from the student's home language to the new language.

Languages, with their complex implications for identity, communication, social integration, education and development, are of strategic importance for people and the planet. Yet, due to globalisation processes, some are increasingly under threat, or disappearing altogether. When languages fade, so does the world's rich tapestry of cultural diversity. Opportunities, traditions, memory, unique modes of thinking and expression – valuable resources for ensuring a better future – are also lost. UNESCO celebrates 21 February as International Mother Language Day to promote linguistic and cultural diversity and multilingualism.

## Teacher standards

EAL is mentioned specifically in Teacher Standard 5: Adapt teaching to respond to the strengths and needs of all pupils (DfE, 2012b). There is relevance to teaching and learning for EAL learners in two of the elements:

- Know when and how to differentiate appropriately, using approaches which enable pupils to be taught effectively.

- Have a clear understanding of the needs of all pupils, including those with special educational needs; those of high ability; those with English as an additional language; and those with disabilities – and be able to use and evaluate distinctive teaching approaches to engage and support them.

## Bilingualism in Wales

Estyn (cited in National Assembly for Wales Commission, 2010) defines bilingualism as the ability to speak, read and write in two languages. In Wales, bilingualism relates to Welsh and English as the official languages of Wales. 'When we inspect bilingualism, we look at learners' achievement in Welsh and English and the extent to which providers promote and develop learners' bilingual skills' (Jones, 2017).

A national poet of Wales, Ifor Ap Glyn, quotes a saying in Welsh, 'cenedl heb iaith, cenedl heb galon' ('A nation without a language is a nation without a heart'), and believes that 'the Welsh language is still very much at the heart of our national culture' (Glyn, n.d.).

A Welsh Government document, 'Taking Wales Forward 2016–21', details its plans to revive Welsh as the national language; the Government is providing children with opportunities to learn Welsh and is aiming for the language to be spoken by a million speakers by 2050 (Jones, 2016).

The Welsh Government aims to enable all learners to gain confidence in their Welsh language skills and enjoy learning and teaching that inspires them. The Welsh in Education: Action Plan 2017–21 (Wales Education, 2017) includes the following five objectives: curriculum, assessment and pedagogy; enrichment and experiences in Welsh; workforce planning, professional learning and leadership; planning Welsh medium education; and excellence, equity and well-being.

Teachers in Wales teach children from different backgrounds – children who speak English as a first language, and children who speak Welsh as a first language. This results in children having different proficiencies in Welsh and English. Few lessons are taught in just Welsh or English; they use a strategic bilingual approach, for example code switching (alternating between both languages as they teach), targeted translation (where specific terms or passages are translated as they are taught), or translanguaging (blending two languages together to help students learn in both languages), to ensure better understanding.

## ● CASE STUDY: A SETTING MEETING THE NEEDS OF DIVERSE FAMILIES (CULTURALLY AND LINGUISTICALLY)

A childcare setting provides admission to young children from refugee families. In order to meet the needs of these children from different backgrounds who are bi- or multilinguals speaking languages other than English, practitioners use a wide range of resources in different languages. The setting has a policy that encourages all practitioners to work closely with each other to share good practice and to resolve issues related to meeting the needs of children and families. Practitioners visit families to familiarise themselves with the child's needs before the child starts nursery. There will be opportunities to gather information about family members and relationships and languages spoken by family members and the child – including their proficiency in English and a list of basic words in their mother tongue such as 'toilet' (or the word used by the child to indicate his or her urge to visit the toilet), 'hunger', 'drink' (or water specifically), 'yes', 'no', (signs), 'hot' and 'cold'. This information can be displayed for use by all the practitioners who will need to work with different children who cannot speak English and/or have limited speaking abilities.

## ACTIVITIES AND RESOURCES

Below is an activity for practitioners in childcare settings to work on together for 30 minutes on a weekly basis to share good practice and resolve barriers.

Table 4.2 could be developed by encouraging practitioners to fill in their details.

Table 4.2: Practitioners' strengths, resources and experience of diversity

| Name of the practitioner | Languages known | Experience of visiting different countries | Familiarity with different cultures | Strengths |
|---|---|---|---|---|
| | | | | |

## Reflection point

How does this relate to children who are not able to use verbal language, use sign language, or with restricted verbal language due to disabilities?

## Simple strategies and resources

- A table showing the profile of language diversity relating to the language proficiencies of practitioners and families can be developed in the settings. How could new languages be introduced to children in their daily routine?

- Focus on the strengths of family members – bi- or multilingual, story telling, creative activities; involve them in activities working with children and/or supporting practitioners in the childcare setting. Parents who can speak languages other than English can help the setting to translate simple phrases and display them across the setting. Parents can be encouraged to support activities related to communication and language.

- Encourage parents to locate their origin on a world map (displayed on the wall) with a pin and indicate their proficiencies (at speaking, reading and writing) in different languages. Share any resources such as books, stories and songs in different languages and collaborate with the teacher or practitioner.

- Small groups of parents may compile nursery rhymes, stories, etc. in their mother tongue/home languages from their countries and English and produce bilingual books that can be used for and by children supported by their practitioners and/or teachers.

- Allow EAL learners thinking time. EAL learners need time to process what is being said and time to formulate a response. Use an appropriate facial expression, tone of voice and body language (gestures, quick mimes) to enhance the meaning.

- All languages can be valued by the settings by asking the children speaking different languages to say a simple word or sentence in their own/first language. Children can be language ambassadors or buddies, learn to count and name colours and days of the week. Two children speaking different languages can be given joint responsibilities; use pictures as well as words to help children to be familiar with key routines.

- Discuss the origins of language – where it has originated and how it has evolved.

- The countries where the languages are spoken can be identified on the map.

- Expose them to different languages and different writing systems.

- Welcome signs and key information in different languages of the community can be used.

- Encourage different languages to be used and heard in classrooms, corridors and the playground.

- Parents and staff should be open to different languages.

- Children's favourite stories can be translated into different languages and displayed.

- Ensure the library has multilingual resources.

- Resources could include bilingual books; encourage parents to lend or donate books from various cultures, languages and traditions, and discuss the characters and relevance in contemporary contexts.

## USE OF BILINGUAL BOOKS IN A SETTING

A bilingual story book narrates a story in two languages. The bilingual book can be sent home a few days before the story is read to everyone in the group. The parent can read the story book to the child in their mother tongue and encourage the child to be familiar with the story. This will enable the child to understand the story better when it is read by the teacher and enables the child to participate in story time and further helps them to learn words and phrases in the English language or other languages. Some commercial companies offer a wide range of resources such as traditional books, interactive audio books, CDs and learning materials in multiple languages.[2]

Teaching for Change[3] suggests that books for children must avoid stereotypes, discriminatory language, tokenism and negative judgements for specific groups. Encouraging children to be colour-blind may increase biases to different races and promote positive messages about diversity.

Books that reflect different cultures and portray children from diverse backgrounds enable children to gain an insight to others' lives as well as reinforcing their own perspectives. Research done in the USA and the UK has raised concerns about the lack of representation of non-White characters as the main characters in story books.

The lack of representation has been reported in children's books published in the UK (Flood, 2018; Ramdarshan Bold, 2019). Arts Council England and the Centre for Literacy in Primary Education (CLPE) are evaluating the extent of and quality of representation of characters from ethnic minority groups.

---

2   www.alien-languages.com, www.languagelizard.com
3   www.teachingforchange.org

CLPE (2019), in their report titled 'Reflecting Realities – Survey of Ethnic Representation within UK Children's Literature 2018', indicated that there has been a slight increase in books that included BAME characters from 4 per cent in 2017 to 7 per cent in 2018, as well as main characters from 1 per cent to 4 per cent. The BAME characters represented small roles with negative characters. CLPE believed that this did not reflect the BAME population in the UK and recommended that BAME characters must be represented in a positive manner.

Technology plays an important part in supporting teachers to communicate with new EAL children and their parents who do not speak much English. For example, translation software such as Google Translate and Google speaker buttons have been used by a primary school in the Netherlands, which has children belonging to more than 90 nationalities and speaking over 60 different languages. Martin and McCracken (2018) from the International School of the Hague (ISH) have shared their success using Google Translate with older children and Google speaker buttons with Key Stage 1 and Foundation Stage children. Google speaker buttons have been used to enable children (EAL and native speakers) to communicate and enhance their social interactions and play experiences. Although the authors referred to both advantages and disadvantages, they indicated that Google speaker buttons have allowed the children to learn and communicate with a child with EAL. Thus, they can make learning a new language a reality even for the youngest children.

## Reflection points

What about those schools with predominantly monolingual pupils, especially English-speaking ones? How do you ensure the children and staff are exposed to different languages?

Will an EAL teacher have a positive impact on the child's achievement?

## Practitioner tips

Practitioners should try to familiarise the words for the following in the child's mother tongue before a young child starts nursery or school:

- greetings

- toilet questions

- drink

- snack

- hungry

- yes/no.

Practitioners have to be aware of certain pronunciations or spelling mistakes made by diverse children and their families, as they may not have learnt from native speakers or they may not be aware of certain syllables or letters. For example, an Arabic speaker may replace a word starting with a 'p' with a 'b'. For children to grow in confidence in language, their environment must reflect their cultural and linguistic heritage and support their learning by providing a wide range of stimuli and experiences.

One of the biggest dilemmas is whether it is appropriate for a child to speak in their first language when they start attending a pre-school in an English majority. Can children learn two languages at the same time?

There are different opinions about respecting children's right to speak their home language in early childhood settings and respecting parents' wishes about their children speaking only in English so that they learn English from native speakers (Hu, Torr and Whiteman, 2014). Some parents prefer their children to speak in English in early childhood settings, whereas others feel their child should be allowed to speak their mother tongue. Encouraging children to use their home language or mother tongue will enable children to develop cognitive and socioemotional skills, as well as developing their language skills.

## Some key points from the chapter

×   Multilingualism is becoming the norm due to migration of population for a wide range of reasons. However, monolingualism is still common in some rich industrialised countries, such as the USA, Australia, the UK, etc.

×   Inclusion is high on the agenda of several Northern countries, involving stakeholders at different levels, from government (policy makers) to the local level (early childhood settings), and include children and families from different backgrounds speaking different languages.

×   Research has shown that children are capable of learning more than one language, and it has recommended that bilingual children must have opportunities to speak in their mother tongue.

×   There is lots of evidence pointing to the impact of learning different languages at an early age. However, some settings consider the diverse languages spoken by children and their families to be a threat.

×   Good practice and strategies used in settings related to bi- or multilingualism should be shared between practitioners in schools and early childhood settings.

×   Early childhood settings should work with children and their (immediate and extended) families to share resources such as stories, nursery rhymes and creative activities using words from different languages.

# 5

## Intersectionality

This chapter will focus on:

- the concept, definitions and perspectives of intersectionality

- theories influencing intersectionality

- issues and controversies around intersectionality

- criticism

- reflections and experiences.

## TERMS, CONCEPTS AND CONTROVERSIES

### INTERSECTIONALITY – KEY IDEAS

- proposed/developed by Kimberlé Crenshaw (1989)

- one of the fastest-travelling concepts (Alanen, 2016)

- a buzzword (Davis, 2008)

- widely adopted and applied, especially in feminist/gender studies

- extended to inter- and multi-disciplinary studies such as disability studies, race studies and human rights studies

- a multi-faceted and open-ended concept (Marfelt, 2016).

## Some definitions, concepts and perspectives

Intersectionality is a term coined by Kimberlé Crenshaw in 1989 to explain the oppression experienced by African American women and highlighting the intersection of race and sex. However, the concept was initially developed in the seventies by a group of Black feminist scholars, who named their group Combahee River Collective and released a statement that explored intersecting oppression (1977).

Intersectionality is an umbrella term which can identify different sorts of relationships between categories (Lykke, 2010). The value attached to these categories are influenced by societal, political, economic and social processes (Lykke, 2010). Lykke also suggests that intersectionality is a concept about societal inclusion/exclusion and dominance/subordination.

Intersectionality refers to the 'interaction between gender, race, and other categories of difference in individual lives, social practices, institutional arrangements, and cultural ideologies and the outcomes of these interactions in terms of power' (Davis, 2008, p.68).

Intersectionality also implies that an individual experiences multiple discrimination related to all categories he or she is associated with simultaneously. The discrimination can be positive or negative depending on how the categories are constructed in the context of society. An individual is identified based on several categories, which may be visible or invisible. The identity of an individual is influenced by the context in which the person lives. Some of these categories are acknowledged to be positive, while others may be seen to be not valued as much at face value. This will be especially true if the individual identifies with several marginalised groups and may be discriminated against and face prejudice due to their place in the hierarchy of status and power. Intersectionality assumes that discrimination is not static and that a person's different identities are subjected to discrimination depending on time, situation and location (la Rivière Zijdel, 2009, p.34).

An individual's identity can be referred to a wide range of categories such as their race, ethnicity, culture, gender, language, social class, education, religion, ability and sexuality. If an individual identifies with more than one category that is recognised as a poor status, minority or marginalised group in the context of a country, then an intersection of these categories might result in being discriminated against and they might perhaps face intersectional discrimination.

Intersectionality considers an individual's position from the perspective of multiple axes of difference, rather than from one single axis, such as race or gender. Brah and Phoenix (2004) highlight the multiple perspectives of an individual's identity and refer to 'intersectionality' as signifying the complex, irreducible, varied and variable effects which ensue when multiple axes of differentiation – economic, political, cultural, psychic, subjective and experiential – intersect in historically specific contexts.

Intersectionality is about inequality experienced, and the power dynamics influencing the interaction of different categories such as race, class and gender. It is important to acknowledge the inter-group and intra-group differences in the identity categories that are integrated within and across critical social and cultural contexts (Crenshaw, 1991; Hill-Collins, 2000).

Intersectionality is an inductive, bottom-up concept, derived from the everyday observation and analysis of routine practices and social positioning, rather than imposed from the top-down by a single discipline or theorist (Phoenix, 2010).

> Intersectionality initiates a process of discovery, alerting us to the fact that the world around us is always more complicated and contradictory than we ever could have anticipated... it encourages complexity, stimulates creativity, and avoids premature closure. (Davis, 2008, p.79)

## INTERSECTIONALITY AND CHILDREN

Children's belonging is related to multiple and intersecting facets of their identities (countries, nationalities, language and social class). Yuval-Davis suggested that belonging is about how people relate to their position regarding their gender, race, ethnicity, social class, age, sexuality and acceptance as part of everyday life (Yuval-Davis, 2006, 2011).

Yuval-Davis (2006, 2011) acknowledged the ways in which children relate to their identities that lead to their belonging (or non-belonging) in their schools. Children develop their 'belonging' to individual groups in abstract or concrete ways, especially by self-identification and also how others identify them.

Haavind and colleagues (2015) questioned the tensions around dual identification of individuals and how they relate to several categories and identify themselves in different contexts. Further, individuals who relate to multiple categories face conflicts in relation to their identity and which one they belong to, as it might change according to the context. Haavind and colleagues found that when Chinese girls were with their Chinese-speaking friends, they felt they belonged, and when they were with English-speaking friends, they experienced exclusion, believing that 'they' (others) do not like Chinese girls.

Kustatscher (2017) suggested that an intersectional lens will allow better understanding of the complex links between identities, power and spaces of belonging. She believed that emotions contributed to how intersectional identities influenced children's peer relationships. She suggested that an intersectional lens will allow an understanding of the complex links between identities, power and spaces of belonging.

## THEORETICAL BASE

Davis (2008) believes that although intersectionality is influenced by feminist theory, the concept is still confusing. It is unclear if intersectionality is considered to be a theory, concept or heuristic device, and as a strategy for doing feminist analysis (Davis, 2008). Konstantoni and Emejulu (2017) challenged the concept of intersectionality. They indicated that few sources (or literature) made explicit references to a theoretical or methodological framework or a praxis, and they also believed that the Black feminist origins of intersectionality had been overlooked.

Crenshaw (2004) used intersectionality in the context of feminism by relating to the negative experiences of a Black woman. She suggested that these experiences cannot be understood by separating gender and race as they interact with each other. Crenshaw, in an interview, explains the experiences of a Black woman and conceptualises that 'intersectionality simply came from the idea that if you're standing in the path of multiple forms of exclusion, you are likely to get hit by both. These women are injured, but when the race ambulance and the gender ambulance arrive at the scene, they see these women of colour lying in the intersection and they say, "Well, we can't figure out if this was just race or just sex discrimination. And unless they can show us which one it was, we can't help them."' This determines that a Black woman can be discriminated against based on her colour and gender. If an individual is attached to several categories, there will be more layers of discrimination.

Critical theory refers to how individuals who are oppressed by relating to several categories such as race, sex, sexuality, ability and class are connected and not separate. Collins (2000) quoted Do Bois, who theorised that race, class and nationality are considered to be not just the personal identity of African Americans, but their social hierarchies that shaped them to access their status, poverty and power. Further, intersectionality adds additional layers of complexity to understandings of social inequality and is rarely caused by a single factor. Using intersectionality as an analytic tool encourages us to move beyond seeing social inequality through race-only or class-only lenses.

Intersectionality is interpreted differently in the USA and the UK. For example, American scholars highlight how the system or structure influences the formation of identity. However, in the UK, the focus is on dynamic and relational aspects of social identity.

## Reflection points: Intersectionality

- Lack of an absolute universal definition.

- Several authors referred to categories such as race, gender, etc. The list of the categories considered and the importance of each of these categories has been debated. Yuval-Davis (2006, 2011) warns that all the categories may not be perceived as equal and prioritised in different contexts. There could be tensions due to some of the categories of differences being obvious and other categories may be overlooked.

- Are children categorised based on subjective assessment of the child's abilities or are people influenced by their own assumptions of different categories that a child is linked to? For example, a Black boy who speaks English as an additional language might be expected to perform poorly in academic subjects.

- The impact of the intersections of SEN/disability and EAL are also influencing the outcomes of children in addition to race/ethnicity, gender and class. If an individual relates to more minority categories, does this individual get oppressed?

- Intersectionality has been considered to be a buzzword.

- Intersectionality conceptualises multiple and shifting identities that address difference and diversity.

- Categories vary in different contexts. How are these categories linked to a child in a positive or negative manner? The impact of the differences that intersect with the identity of an individual and experience might vary in different contexts. An Asian disabled girl in the UK can face discrimination and restricted ability to exercise her power, resulting in being oppressed. Bias, norms, judgements and values might be entrenched in society and influences how the categories of difference intersect with each other.

## ISSUES AND CONTROVERSIES

In England there is evidence of blatant discrimination towards children and families who identify themselves as belonging to Gypsy, Roma and Traveller family heritage. The DfE (2018) reported that special educational needs are most prevalent in travellers of Irish heritage (30.9%) and Gypsy/Roma pupils (26.8%) respectively. Travellers of Irish heritage and Black Caribbean pupils had the highest percentage of pupils with statements or EHC plans (4.5% and 4.2% respectively). The most common primary type of need for Mixed (23.3%), Asian (34.0%), Black (31.8%) and Chinese (45.1%) ethnic groups was speech, language and communication needs. A Black Caribbean boy eligible for free school meals who also has special educational needs (SEN) is 168 times more likely to be permanently excluded than a White British girl without SEN and not eligible for free school meals (Connolly, 2012).

Race, ethnicity and special educational needs have been

considered by professionals and policy makers in isolation in providing appropriate provision for children from BME (Black Minority Ethnic) backgrounds. Do all children with special educational needs have homogenous needs? Would a child from a BME background face similar barriers to a non-BME child? Is the barrier caused by the ethnicity or SEN, or a combination of both?

Newly Qualified Teacher (NQT) surveys for several years reported that a significant number of NQTs were not confident to teach children from ethnic minority backgrounds as well as children with special educational needs and EAL (see Chapter 4). The references made to children with special educational needs and children from ethnic minorities in the NQT surveys were considered separately. A child from a BME background with special educational needs may be given a label as a result of inappropriate methods of assessment and assessments in English which may not be suitable due to the child's unfamiliarity with English. Hick (2007) reported that institutional racism resulted in a large number of children from BME backgrounds with SEN labels. He believed 'that minority communities were missing out on important educational opportunities by being labelled as SEN or [by] having their needs overlooked' (p.131).

El Sharif (2010) believed that one of the barriers to inclusion of BME children with SEN could be the more limited contribution of their parents to discussions with professionals in their child's assessments and to decisions about the appropriate provision for them. BME children labelled as having SEN may not be achieving well in their schools, resulting in poor opportunities in their future.

Parents of children from ethnic minority groups may face barriers, such as lack of awareness about expectations and difficulty accessing available services due to barriers associated with language and culture related to not challenging the authority of professionals. They may question their own ability to make decisions and to express their views on appropriate provision for their children clearly and confidently. This might ultimately result in exclusion, poor retention, poor achievement and perhaps a low-paid job (Ofsted, 2014; Page and Whitting, 2007).

This shows how a combination of intersections of different categories will influence the experiences of, for example, Black disabled students and how the combination of race/racism and disability/ableism will have an impact on their achievement and success in their future. It has been widely reported that White boys from disadvantaged families have been (Evans, 2016; Weale and Adams, 2016).

Crenshaw (1989) criticised the notion of identity based on a single category. Women perceived through an intersectional lens are not just women but Black, White, rich and poor. Women are situated in positions of privilege or being oppressed based on how their differences are related to in their particular society. All the differences do not interact in a linear fashion and independently of each other. They influence the individual's identity by weaving across and between the various categories. It will be possible to observe the differences that exist between the individuals. Individual, multiple or intersecting sources of oppression, subordination and disadvantage are not directly visible and/or observable and thus can result in the individual being discriminated against and excluded. Sometimes, this could be unintentional and unconscious.

It has been found that girls outperform boys at all levels including the EYFS consistently since 2013 (DfE, 2017). The family, school and neighbourhood in which children live all contribute to their development and well-being. The inequalities associated with race and gender are a result of bias and discrimination at structural (institutional) and individual (practitioner) levels.

Bécares and Priest (2015) reported that Black girls score much lower than White boys in Maths assessments. This difference, not explained by intrinsic or socioeconomic differences, can be contextualised as a result of experienced intersecting racial and gender discrimination. The consequences of the intersection between two marginalised identities are found throughout the results of this study when comparing across broad categorisations of race/ethnicity and gender, and in more detailed conceptualisations of minority status. Growing up Black, Latino or White in the USA is not the same for boys and girls, and growing up as a boy or a girl in America does not lead to the same outcomes and opportunities for Black, Latino and White children as they become adults.

The impact of the intersections of SEN/disability and EAL is also influencing the outcomes of children in addition to race/ethnicity, gender and class. If an individual relates to more categories, does this individual get oppressed and discriminated against? Bécares and Priest (2015) report that the intersections of racial/ethnic and gender discrimination have a detrimental effect on the academic outcomes of eighth grade students (13–14-year-olds) that has an impact on their success in adult life.

The impact of the intersections of SEN/disability and EAL is also influencing the outcomes of children in addition to race/ethnicity, gender and class. If an individual relates to more categories, does this individual get more oppressed and discriminated against?

## ISSUES FOR SETTINGS, CHILDREN AND FAMILIES

There has been a steady increase in the number of children from ethnic minority groups in England. In primary schools, 33.1 per cent of pupils of school age are of minority ethnic origins, an increase from 32.1 per cent in January 2017. In secondary schools, 30.3 per cent of pupils are of minority ethnic origins, an increase from 29.1 per cent in 2017 (DfE, 2018).

A child from a family of asylum seekers might be discriminated against on the basis of their gender, how they look different, their proficiency in English, their lack of familiarity with local culture, abilities and background. Every individual has multiple identities irrespective of their background. These categories of differences might have a different effect on children in different contexts. If a child is in a minority category for several aspects of their identity, such as ethnicity, religion, language, etc., then there is a possibility that the child will face discrimination and lack of ability to exercise their power.

How do children respond to children from different backgrounds from their own? Below is an example of my reflections on meeting a child from a Black and minority ethnic background.

## ● CASE STUDY

I visited an early childhood setting on the pretext of visiting a student in the setting.

Before meeting the child – The manager of the setting was concerned about a three-year-old Asian boy, Mani (pseudonym), in the nursery. I was told that this child had arrived with his family in England in the last few weeks and had been attending the setting for a couple of weeks. Mani was not participating in any activities, despite all the strategies used by the staff to enable the child to settle in. On the contrary, the child was not communicating at all, and was distressed, crying and withdrawn from all children and activities.

Observation and initial interaction with Mani – Visibly terrified but within seconds he seems to have raised hopes, perhaps a result of seeing somebody with a similar skin colour in the nursery. After starting a conversation in a few languages (hoping that communication in his native language might help) for just 30 seconds, Mani seemed a little excited and started talking fluently in his native language (which sounded very different to all the languages I had tried to speak). He surprised me by holding my hand and walked me to the coat stand in the nursery and showed his coat and bag and, almost like a request and order, said 'Let's go home' (in his native language, I had guessed – his nonverbal communication indicated that's what he meant). Momentarily I could not believe his proposal (as I was a total stranger, who had met him only a few minutes before). Trying to help, I asked about the location of the house and feigned innocence on not being aware of how to get to his house. He retorted immediately (with more excitement), 'Easy, change two buses and the house is on the road.' Mani's confidence in me threw me off the ground and I was dumbstruck on how to help this child and the setting.

## SOME REFLECTIONS

Did the practitioners in the setting believe that there was an invisible barrier between them, that led them to believe that the child was difficult to include because of visible differences? This shows how a predominantly White setting might have struggled to meet the needs of a three-year-old child. Do the practitioners lack confidence in meeting the needs of children from ethnic minorities? Is it due to poor knowledge and understanding due to a lack of adequate training?

Intersectionality – The above situation seems to suggest that the child is at a disadvantage due to his race and his inability to speak the English language. Staff indicated that they were not successful in helping Mani to settle down despite all their efforts. In addition, Mani did not feel comfortable with strangers who looked different and spoke an unknown and unfamiliar language. On the other hand, he developed an instant connection with a total stranger almost immediately due to similarities in skin colour and physical features, although Mani and I spoke totally different languages. Despite the best intentions and efforts of the staff, Mani experienced exclusion and disadvantage. There was evidence of Mani's struggle in developing his identity and demonstrating his confidence to relate to strangers in different contexts. Lack of a peer group with a similar background in the early childhood setting may lead to the child feeling apprehensive and intimidated, resulting in them self-segregating despite the setting making attempts to include the child.

The child did not feel he belonged in the setting as the staff in the setting struggled to relate to the needs of a newly arrived child. Their lack of knowledge and understanding and limited exposure to diversity resulted in not providing access to the rights of the child and not valuing the child's strengths.

Another observation concerns a seven-year-old White girl named Betty (pseudonym) who attended with a high proportion of Black children. When a group of young White female students visited Betty's class, she ran and hugged one of them immediately.

This shows that, although Betty attended a school where English was spoken and she lived in an English-speaking country, she was conscious that the majority of the children in her school were from different ethnic groups and looked different to her.

It is important to ensure that all early childhood settings, whether they serve diverse communities or not, make use of resources which offer positive representations of diverse groups of people.

## Reflection point: Dilemmas of a child

Nalini, a four-year-old Indian girl living in England with her parents (first generation migrants), expressed her dilemma to her mother: 'Mum, will I be an English lady when I grow up?' This raises a few questions around identity such as:

- What is the context of this question?

- Would she like to be an English lady when she grows up? This might sound illogical and unrealistic to the adult.

- Does she expect that she will grow into an English lady because she is living in England? Would she like to become an English lady when she grows up?

- Is she wishing to become an English lady so that she will be accepted by her peers?

- What are the reasons for Nalini's dilemmas, conflicts and tensions? Are these a result of discussions with the peer group or a circle time activity based on identity or secretly wishing her skin colour will change?

- How is the concept of 'English lady' related to skin colour, posh clothes or other perspectives?

This seems to relate to the numerous issues influencing an individual's identity or multiple identities that may be visible or invisible. For example, facial features, skin colour, hair colour and dress (influenced by their own culture or religion) might be visible, and accent, abilities, beliefs and values are invisible, but still influence the individual's identity. If a child is from a mixed heritage family, will it have other implications for the child's identity? What is the impact if the identity determined by the self matches or does not match with how others perceive the child?

The following examples show that children need familiarity with the backgrounds of people (children and adults), language and culture to feel included and comfortable. A mix of categories that they do not feel familiar with may result in them feeling uncomfortable and perhaps discriminated against. Children may feel intimidated more than adults due to lacking the confidence to assert themselves and project their identity in a positive way.

A three-year-old child from a refugee family from Syria might have several labels attached that they may not identify with. But as a young child, the child is unable to challenge these stereotypes which may be based on gender, ability to speak English, poor family and lack of abilities to be independent. This child might not have any role models or any representation in the resources used, stories read, displays on the walls and diversity in the background of staff members. Some of the key characteristics attached to the child by the adults working with them might be a result of subconscious or unconscious stereotypes that may be a result of how children or adults from these regions are projected with positive or negative representation in different forms of media. What is the impact of this experience on the child's development?

In some communities, there are strong messages influencing domination, oppression and marginalisation around gender, race, ethnicity, class, culture and religion that reinforce stereotypes and prejudices against children from minority communities and their families. Individual identities might be developed and constructed at the crossroads of different axes of social difference and inequality, and these positions are not static and might be a place of constant struggle and negotiation.

## ● PERSONAL EXPERIENCES OF INTERSECTIONS OF DIFFERENCES IMPACTING ON MY IDENTITY

'Who am I?' is a question that I never considered until I moved to England. The differences in expectations related to the categories I was attached to, such as my gender, the region I belonged to, religion and home language or mother tongue. The intersections of these differences seem to have influenced others' expectations for me and enabled me to establish my identity as Indian (that was not contested and not threatened). On the other hand, being recognised as being

British in certain contexts (when filling forms, or international travel or conferences) is also experienced. On a visit to Europe, a colleague commented: '…when you were talking I saw a Briton rather than an Indian…' Does this comment mean that this colleague's perception of my identity changed after meeting me?

Intersections of difference relate to mainly skin colour and facial features in addition to gender, religion and English as an additional language. The impact of these differences seems to vary in different contexts. When I arrived in England, there were questions around my perspectives of identity being Indian or British. The expectations of others, especially about my ability to speak English, was influenced by the stereotype that migrants may have poor English proficiency, partly due to their accent. I often heard comments such as 'Oh, you speak good English'. Could this be a 'microaggression', which Sue and colleagues (2007, p.108) describe as 'insidious, damaging, and harmful forms of racism…[that occur] everyday, [and are] unintentional, and unconscious are perpetrated by ordinary citizens who believe they are doing right'?

Close friends, who are work colleagues and from the neighbourhood, acknowledged my identity as Indian and also British. These were people who were familiar with me for a long time. Some people redefined their perceptions.

My identity in India again had some contradictions and confusion, mainly due to how I would present myself as Indian rather than British, especially with my preference to wear Indian rather than Western dresses. Confusion and conflict is mainly a result of not fully fitting into the typical Indian stereotype – especially when speaking English.

Discrimination is not just based on colour, but visible and explicit labels such as disability might influence another person's perceptions. Below is the perspective of an individual who is from the UK and White; she has shared her experiences of tensions and conflicts related to her identity.

Fiona (pseudonym), an ex-student, is a young adult who has completed her degree. She shares her perspectives on her identity and has been reflecting on the intersectionality of different categories related to her identity, such as her disability, Welshness and gender in the context of living in England and Wales.

This is her perspective of the different categories that she can relate to impacting on her identity and of her struggles dealing with negative experiences due to discrimination, as well as some positive experiences which supported her to develop a positive identity through intersectionality of all the categories she can relate to.

## CASE STUDY OF A YOUNG PRACTITIONER (IN HER OWN WORDS)

As an individual, my identity centres greatly around my Welsh upbringing. With my family being predominantly Welsh and my upbringing and growing up in Wales, I find being Welsh as being critical to respecting my culture and maintaining a subconscious relationship with my community and family background. Being Welsh is an essential part of who I am as an individual and is a link with a place which forms much of my personality, characteristics and thinking. This was influenced by both my educational experiences prior to university and the Welshness shared with my family. Much of my educational experience focused on Welsh culture, with this being a shared commonality amongst the school, whereby the Welsh language and celebrations were promoted amongst provision, creating a strong community within Welsh foundations.

I found it to be frustrating when identified as English or another nationality, or if there was a misconception about my upbringing, as this felt unnatural to how I subconsciously identified myself. Yet, I found it challenging to correct an individual as I was perhaps concerned about feeling awkward or boastful.

Expanding upon my identity, my physical condition, Achondroplasia, has become more associated with my identity as I have developed, which I believe to be encouraged through the comments, perspectives and thoughts of others. Whereas family and friends viewed me as an individual regardless of the condition, it became more apparent to others as I matured.

As a child, I found much of my educational experiences to be highly inclusive and understanding, greatly supported by a parent–partnership approach held between the staff and my parents, encouraging a fairer approach to practice. Although, in later adolescence I found more offensive engagements to occur, particularly with name-calling and the changes in facial expressions when in public, including staring and moments of bullying focused on my condition from staff, children, peers and the public. These experiences made it more apparent that I was visibly different to a degree. It influenced the perspectives of others, often negatively, and influenced my confidence in my appearance.

The possible influence of such negative attitudes could derive from the lack of positive imagery in practice reflecting diversity, including those with a physical difference. I believe it is also encouraged by the pre-conceived fears of others to be associated with others with a difference or to not wish to cause offence through limited knowledge, particularly when an individual may hold a distinct difference in comparison to the majority.

As a result, this influenced my professional perspective to incorporate more open practice, whereby I recognise perceived stereotypes do not guarantee an accurate, holistic overview of an individual and their capabilities or potential. Although a negative experience, it contained a positive influence upon my practice to take part in limiting the domino effect in early years practice, whereby stereotypes and limited judgements must be lowered to open the potential and opportunities of individuals and their sense of identity, where difference is looked at positively.

Gender, ethnicity and disability are the three key attributes influencing Fiona's identity. Does her self-identity differ from how she is seen by others? Is it due to the visible nature of her disability? What attributes are visible to others that have led to Fiona's negative experiences? The intersections of categories of disability, Welshness and gender have had positive and negative influences on Fiona's self-esteem and developing self-identity.

As suggested in the wheel of inclusion (see Figure I.2 in the Introduction), identifying and appreciating (or emphasising) Fiona's strengths consistently would have enabled the wheel of inclusion to accelerate and resulted in positive experiences. She has had both positive and negative experiences due to lack of awareness and stereotypes reinforced in the settings and schools.

## MEN IN EARLY CHILDHOOD EDUCATION

The workforce in early childhood education is predominantly female, and is stereotypically feminine, professionally undervalued and underpaid (Moss, 2006). Several discussions and discourses strongly oppose the idea of males as early childhood practitioners to be problematic (Warin, 2019; Weale, 2019). This is highlighted as a global phenomenon supported by the number of male practitioners in different countries. Poor achievement of boys at different levels has been attributed to the high numbers of female education professionals at early years and primary levels (Lloyd, 2011). This points to the fact that issues such as poor status and poor pay, which stereotypically are considered not acceptable to men, may have led to them not being interested in childcare jobs (Lloyd, 2018).

There are conflicting ideas around men as early childhood practitioners, as in some cases they have not been accepted by society (especially parents of young children), but governments have been attempting to improve the participation and involvement of males. This led to males being positioned as 'wanted other', as several governments, especially in developed countries, are actively engaged in recruiting men into early childhood settings.

In several countries it has been reported that men (as professionals and fathers) are not considered appropriate to provide a caring role due to lack of skills and competencies (Sak *et al.*, 2019). In developed countries, a male who is also from an ethnic minority group such as Asian or Black might be considered suspicious and dangerous as an early childhood professional. In this context, a male who is interested in this career might face discrimination because of his gender difference and also his ethnicity. Children will benefit from having a male role model, particularly those from single mother families. This is especially relevant for young boys to develop their personality and socioemotional developments (Warin, 2018).

## ACTIVITY

Encourage children in the classroom to discuss and identify the categories relevant to their personal perspective.

Discuss and make a note of the key differences and their impact on the children.

### WHO AM I?

In a circle time activity, encourage the children and practitioners to discuss their perceptions of identity in relation to the following categories:

- gender/sex/sexual orientation

- race/ethnicity

- nationality

- affiliation to a religion/spirituality

- ability.

Are there any conflicts between your perceptions and others in relation to how you are identified and how you would like to be identified? Is anyone confused about their identity, especially being British or feeling White or Black? Consider which identities will put them at an advantage or disadvantage in the context of their immediate society.

## Some key points from the chapter

×  There is a wide range of definitions for intersectionality relating to differences in the categories and experiences of differences in different contexts – negative and tokenistic.

×  Using an intersectional lens not only opens up a view of identities and belonging as multiple and complex, but also crucially draws attention to the power dynamics involved in creating hierarchies, belonging and boundaries (Davis, 2008).

×  This is evident in the ways in which children use emotions to demonstrate their belonging to various places and groups (countries, nationalities, language and social class) which are ascribed different values and status, involving political decisions about who belongs, and who does not (Yuval-Davis, 2011).

×  Intersectionality adds additional layers of complexity to our understanding of social inequality, recognising that social inequality is rarely caused by a single factor. Using intersectionality as an analytic tool encourages us to move beyond seeing social inequality through race-only or class-only lenses. Instead, intersectionality encourages understandings of social inequality based on interactions among various categories.

× Practitioners and professionals may see children through a narrow lens influenced by certain labels and the stereotypes associated with them. This may result in the child's strengths being overlooked and thus impact on the child's holistic development.

# Conclusion

Early childhood settings and schools are increasingly becoming diverse, and practitioners are expected to meet the unique and evolving needs of children. The diversity of practitioners and teachers does not reflect the differences visible in the community. Practitioners and teachers' limited knowledge and understanding of diversity has been highlighted, which resulted in homogenising the needs of all children labelled as belonging to a group. Further, some children and their families were stereotyped, while others with invisible differences may have been overlooked as they appeared similar to the majority of children. This might affect collaboration between the families and settings due to the lack of understanding or misunderstanding of different cultures and lack of awareness of different languages spoken.

The positive interaction between practitioners, teachers from early childhood settings and schools, family and the government is significant to enable children to develop to the best of their potential in all areas of development. Although the engagement of settings and families is direct and almost on a daily basis, the services provided to children through the policies and initiatives of the government are also significant.

Figure C.1 shows the interaction between families, practitioners and settings and the government. The child is in the middle protected by the families, settings and government. As shown in the figure, the impact of government is one sided as policies and legislation are implemented at grassroots level, but in an ideal situation, the interaction between families and settings must be mutual, influencing the services provided for the child.

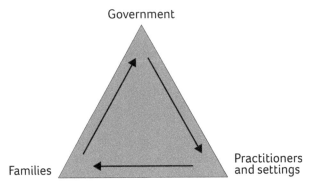

*Figure C.1: Interaction between families, practitioners, settings and the government*

This book has covered some relevant aspects of diversity, such as race and ethnicity, culture, EAL, religion and intersectionality, and discussed key challenges experienced by practitioners and teachers at grassroots (early childhood settings and schools) level and policy makers and politicians at government (local, national), as well as international, level. This chapter concludes the book by summarising some of the positive steps discussed in the book that can be taken to help promote inclusion and diversity.

## POSITIVE PRACTICE

- Technology has been a positive, enabling staff in schools and early childhood settings to access knowledge and understanding of diverse cultures and languages. This will raise awareness and enable them to understand the children and their families better. Success stories can be shared online, which can build networks of practitioners to support each other. Google Translate is popular and is used in early childhood settings and schools to communicate with children and families speaking different languages.

- Settings and practitioners are welcoming towards migrants and are able to empathise with their circumstances due to the coverage of their hardships on a wide range of media platforms.

- The wheel of inclusion model (see the Introduction) will enable practitioners and teachers to focus on the strengths of an individual and enable the individual to overcome their weaknesses. This can be adapted to the local contexts.

- A wide range of resources reflecting the diversity of the population is available in public libraries, as well as on the open market, for settings to access and use with the diverse children they work with. Practitioners must consciously ensure the resources used do not stereotype or prejudice the children from minority groups, but must be confident to challenge stereotypes by discussing them with children.

- Early childhood settings are collaborating with children and their (immediate and extended) families to share resources such as stories, nursery rhymes and creative activities using words from different cultures and languages.

- Using an intersectional lens not only opens up a view of identities and belonging as multiple and complex, but also, crucially, draws attention to the power dynamics involved in creating hierarchies, belonging and boundaries.

# RECOMMENDATIONS

- Provide opportunities for all staff members to discuss their experiences, including confronting their own stereotypes, and to update their knowledge and understanding through frequent training.

- Ensure the setting has a wide range of resources providing positive images reflecting the diversity in the wider community irrespective of the diversity of children in the setting. Resources should reinforce positive messages and role models and avoid negative stereotypes.

- Celebrate different festivals – cultural, religious, important celebrations.

- Be good role models – for positive perspectives and experiences related to diversity and inclusion.

- Respect, acknowledge and celebrate diversity.

- Engage with families (immediate and extended) and community organisations representing minority groups, religions and cultures.

- Provide opportunities for children to share their culture and celebrations.

- Ensure everyone in the school community is celebrated whether it is a multicultural or predominantly monocultural setting.

- Train leaders to embrace diversity and support the staff to develop a positive ethos in the setting.

- Be proactive rather than reactive in meeting the needs of all children by keeping the channels of communication open.

# Bibliography

Aboud, F.E. (2008) 'A Social-Cognitive Developmental Theory of Prejudice.' In S.M. Quintana and C. McKown (eds) *Handbook of Race, Racism, and the Developing Child*. New Jersey: John Wiley & Sons Inc.

Adler, P. (1974) 'Beyond cultural identity: Reflections on cultural and multicultural man.' *Topics in Culture and Learning 2*, 23–40.

Advance HE (2019) 'Use of language: Race and ethnicity.' Retrieved from www.advance-he.ac.uk/guidance/equality-diversity-and-inclusion/using-data-and-evidence/use-of-language-race-ethnicity on 26/02/20.

Ainscow, M., Dyson, A., Hopwood, L. and Thomson, S. (2016) *Primary Schools Responding to Diversity: Barriers and Possibilities*. York: Cambridge Primary Review Trust.

Alanen, L. (2016) '"Intersectionality" and other challenges to theorizing childhood.' *Childhood 23*, 2, 157–161.

Arnot, M., Schneider, C., Evans, M., Liu, Y., Welply, O. and Davies-Tutt, D. (2014) *School Approaches to the Education of EAL Students: Language Development, Social Integration and Achievement*. Cambridge: The Bell Educational Trust Ltd.

Au, K.H. and Blake, K.M. (2003) 'Cultural identity and learning to teach in a diverse community: Findings from a collective case study.' *Journal of Teacher Education 54*, 3, 192–205.

Bach, D. (2017) 'Bilingual babies: Study shows how exposure to a foreign language ignites infants.' Retrieved from www.washington.edu/news/2017/07/17/bilingual-babies-study-shows-how-exposure-to-a-foreign-language-ignites-infants-learning on 30/01/20.

Banerjee, R. and Luckner, J. (2014) 'Training needs of early childhood professionals who work with children and families who are culturally and linguistically diverse.' *Infants and Young Children 27*, 1, 43–59.

Banks, J. (1988) *Multi-Ethnic Education: Theory and Practice*. Boston, MA: Allyn and Bacon.

Banks, J.A. (2015) *Cultural diversity and education: Foundations, curriculum, and teaching*. Abingdon: Routledge.

Banks, J.A. and Ambrosio, J. (2020) 'Multicultural education.' Retrieved from https://education.stateuniversity.com/pages/2252/Multicultural-Education.html on 26/02/20.

BBC (2017) 'More than half in UK are non-religious, suggests survey.' Retrieved from www.bbc.co.uk/news/uk-41150792 on 30/01/20.

Beauboeuf-Lafontant, T. (1999) 'A movement against and beyond boundaries.' *Teachers College Record 100*, 4, 702–723.

Bécares, L. and Priest, N. (2015) 'Understanding the influence of race/ethnicity, gender, and class on inequalities in academic and non-academic outcomes among eighth-grade students: Findings from an INTERSECTIONALITY APPROACH.' *PLoS ONE 10*, 10, e0141363.

Bell Foundation (2017) 'Education policy in EAL in England.' Retrieved from https://ealresources.bell-foundation.org.uk/eal-specialists/education-policy-eal-england on 30/01/20.

Bhopal, R. (2003) 'Glossary of terms relating to ethnicity and race: For reflection and debate.' *Journal of Epidemiology & Community Health 58*, 441–445.

Billigmeier, R.H. (2016) *A Crisis in Swiss Pluralism: The Romansh and Their Relations with the German- and Italian-Swiss in the Perspective of a Millennium.* The Hague: Mouton Publishers.

Boutte, G.S., Lopez-Robertson, J. and Powers-Costello, E. (2011) 'Moving beyond colorblindness in early childhood classrooms.' *Early Childhood Education Journal 39*, 5, 335.

Brah, A. and Phoenix, A. (2004) 'Ain't I a woman? Revisiting intersectionality.' *Journal of International Women's Studies 5*, 3, 75–86.

Bronson, P. and Merryman, A. (2009) *NurtureShock: New Thinking about Children.* London: Hachette UK.

Brooker, L. and Woodhead, M. (2008) *Developing Positive Identities: Diversity and Young Children* (No. 3). Buckingham: Open University.

Bryce, E. (2020) 'What's the difference between race and ethnicity?' Retrieved from www.livescience.com/difference-between-race-ethnicity.html on 26/02/20.

Bullivant, S. (2018) *Europe's Young Adults and Religion: Findings from the European Social Survey (2014–16) to Inform the 2018 Synod of Bishops.* St Mary's University, Twickenham. London: Benedict XVI Centre for Religion and Society.

Burke, M.M. (2017) 'Examining empowerment, family–school partnerships, and advocacy among rural and urban Latino families of children with disabilities.' *Rural Special Education Quarterly 36*, 2, 56–63.

Byrd, D., Ceacal, Y.R., Felton, J., Nicholson, C., Rhaney, D.M.L., McCray, N. and Young, J. (2017) 'A modern doll study: Self concept.' *Race, Gender & Class 24*, 1/2, 186–202.

Chamot, A.U. and O'Malley, J.M. (1994) *The CALLA Handbook: Implementing the Cognitive Academic Language Learning Approach.* White Plains, MA: Addison Wesley Longman.

Chen, G.M., Starosta, W.J., Lin, D. and You, Z. (1998) *Foundations of Intercultural Communication.* Boston, MA: Allyn and Bacon.

Chibaka, V.F. (2018) *Advantages of Bilingualism and Multilingualism: Multidimensional Research Findings, Multilingualism and Bilingualism.* Beban Sammy Chumbow, IntechOpen. Retrieved from www.intechopen. com/books/multilingualism-and-bilingualism/advantages-of-bilingualism-and-multilingualism-multidimensional-research-findings on 31/01/20.

Children's Community School (2018) 'They are not too young to talk about race.' Retrieved from www.childrenscommunityschool.org/social-justice-resources on 26/02/20.

Clark, K.B. and Clark, M.K. (1939) 'The development of consciousness of self and the emergence of racial identification in Negro preschool children.' *The Journal of Social Psychology 10,* 4, 591–599.

CLPE (2019) 'Reflecting realities – survey of ethnic representation within UK children's literature 2018.' Retrieved from https://clpe.org.uk/publications-and-bookpacks/reflecting-realities/reflecting-realities-survey-ethnic-representation on 31/01/20.

CNN (2010) 'Study: White and Black children biased toward lighter skin.' Retrieved from https://edition.cnn.com/2010/US/05/13/doll.study/index. html on 26/02/20.

Colic-Peisker, V. (2005) '"At least you're the right colour": Identity and social inclusion of Bosnian refugees in Australia.' *Journal of Ethnic and Migration Studies 31,* 4, 615–638.

Collins, P.H. (2000) 'Gender, Black feminism, and Black political economy.' *The Annals of the American Academy of Political and Social Science 568,* 41–53.

Combahee River Collective (1977) 'A Black Feminist Statement.' In L. Nicholson (ed.) *The Second Wave: A Reader in Feminist Theory.* New York: Routledge.

Connolly, J. (2012) 'They never give up on you – the Children's Commissioner's Inquiry into School Exclusions.' *Education Review 24,* 2.

Connolly, P (2002) *Too Young to Notice? The Cultural and Political Awareness of 3–6 Year Olds in Northern Ireland.*

Cooper, V. (2014) 'Children's Developing Identity.' In M. Reed and W. Rosie (eds) *A Critical Companion to Early Childhood.* London: Sage.

CORE (2018) *Final Report. Religion and Worldviews: The Way Forward. A National Plan for RE.* London: Commission on Religious Education.

Cox, K., Tayles, N.G. and Buckley, H.R. (2006) 'Forensic identification of "Race": The issues in New Zealand.' *Current Anthropology,* 2006, 869–874. The University of Chicago Press on behalf of Wenner-Gren Foundation for Anthropological Research Stable. Retrieved from www.jstor.org/stable/10.1086/507187 on 26/02/20.

Crenshaw, K.W. (1989) 'Demarginalizing the intersection of race and sex: A Black feminist critique of antidiscrimination doctrine, feminist theory and antiracist politics.' *The University of Chicago Legal Forum 140,* 139–167.

Crenshaw, K.W. (1991) 'Mapping the margins: Intersectionality, identity politics, and violence against women of color.' *Stanford Law Review 43,* 6, 1241–1299.

Crenshaw, K.W. (2004) 'Intersectionality: The double bind of race and gender.' Interview with Kimberlé Crenshaw, American Bar Association, Spring. Retrieved from www.americanbar.org/content/dam/aba/publishing/perspectives_magazine/women_perspectives_Spring2004CrenshawPSP.authcheckdam.pdf on 26/02/20.

Crisp, T., Knezek, S.M., Quinn, M., Bingham, G.E., Girardeau, K. and Starks, F. (2016) 'What's on our bookshelves? The diversity of children's literature in early childhood classroom libraries.' *Journal of Children's Literature 42,* 2, 29.

Cromarty, H. (2019) House of Commons Library: Briefing Paper Number 08083: 9 May 2019: Gypsies and Travellers.

Cummins, J. (1980) 'The Construct of Language Proficiency in Bilingual Education.' In J.E. Alatis (ed.) *Georgetown University Round Table on Languages and Linguistics.* Washington DC: Georgetown University Press.

Cummins, J. (2005) 'A proposal for action: Strategies for recognizing heritage language competence as a learning resource within the mainstream classroom.' *Modern Language Journal 89,* 585–592.

Cushner, K., McClelland, E. and Safford, P. (1996) *Human Diversity in Education.* New York: McGraw Hill.

Davis, K. (2006) 'A girl like me.' Retrieved from www.youtube.com/watch?v=z0BxFRu_SOw on 26/02/20.

Davis, K. (2008) 'Intersectionality as buzzword: A sociology of science perspective on what makes a feminist theory successful.' *Feminist Theory 9,* 1, 67–85.

Davis, S.C., Leman, P.J. and Barrett, M. (2007) 'Children's implicit and explicit ethnic group attitudes, ethnic group identification, and self-esteem.' *International Journal of Behavioral Development 31,* 5, 514–525.

DCSF (2008) *Early Years Foundation Stage.* Nottingham: DCSF Publications.

DCSF (2009) *Building Futures: Believing in Children. A Focus on Provision for Black Children in the Early Years Foundation Stage.* London: DCSF. Retrieved from https://dera.ioe.ac.uk/8958/7/ey_bca_bldfuture0000809_Redacted.pdf on 26/02/20.

DECET and ISSA (2011) 'Diversity and social inclusion exploring competencies for professional practice for early childhood education and care.' Retrieved from www.issa.nl/sites/default/files/pdf/Publications/equity/Diversity-and-Social-Inclusion_0.pdf on 25/02/20.

Demie, F. (2013) 'English as an additional language pupils: How long does it take to acquire English fluency?' *Language and Education 27,* 1, 59–69.

Department for Education (DfE) (1999) *The national curriculum in England: complete framework for key stages 1 to 4.* Retrieved from http://www.educationengland.org.uk/documents/pdfs/1999-nc-primary-handbook.pdf on 22/06/20.

Department for Education and Skills (DfES) (2006) *Ethnicity and Education: The Evidence on Minority Ethnic Pupils Aged 5–16.* London: DfES.

Derman-Sparks, L. (2008) 'Where are we now – Anti-bias/anti-racism, early childhood and primary education in the USA.' *Race Equality Teaching,* Spring.

Derman-Sparks, L. (2016) 'Guide for selecting anti-bias children's books.' Retrieved from www.teachingforchange.org/selecting-anti-bias-books on 31/01/20.

Derman-Sparks, L. and the ABC Task Force (1989) 'The ABC Task Force.' *Anti-Bias Curriculum: Tools for Empowering Young Children* 3.

Devarakonda, C.S., McGrath, S. and Chaudhary, D. (2019) 'Exploring inclusion and diversity within undergraduate teacher training programmes in England.' EDULEARN19 Proceedings, pp.1947–1955.

DfE (2012a) 'Statutory Framework for the Early Years Foundation Stage: Setting the standards for learning, development and care for children from birth to five.' Retrieved from www.foundationyears.org.uk/files/2014/05/eyfs_statutory_framework_march_2012.pdf on 26/02/20.

DfE (2012b) *The New Teachers' Standards.* London: DfE.

DfE (2013a) *School Uniform: Guidance for Governing Bodies, School Leaders, School Staff and Local Authorities.* London: DfE. Retrieved from www.gov.uk/government/uploads/system/uploads/attachment_data/file/514978/School_Uniform_Guidance.pdf on 26/02/20.

DfE (2013b) *Teachers' Standards: Guidance for School Leaders, School Staff and Governing Bodies.* London: DfE. Retrieved from www.gov.uk/government/publications/teachers-standards on 05/02/20.

DfE (2013c) *Schools, Pupils, and Their Characteristics.* SFR 21/2013. London: DfE.

DfE (2014a) *The National Curriculum in England: Key Stages 3 and 4 Framework Document.* London: DfE. Retrieved from https://assets.publishing.service.gov.uk/government/uploads/system/uploads/attachment_data/file/425601/PRIMARY_national_curriculum.pdf on 05/02/20.

DfE (2014b) *Promoting Fundamental British Values as Part of SMSC in Schools: Departmental Advice for Maintained Schools.* London: DfE. Retrieved from www.gov.uk/government/uploads/system/uploads/attachment_data/file/380595/SMSC_Guidance_Maintained_Schools.pdf on 26/02/20.

DfE (2014c) *School Admissions Code.* London: DfE. Retrieved from https://assets.publishing.service.gov.uk/government/uploads/system/uploads/attachment_data/file/389388/School_Admissions_Code_2014_-_19_Dec.pdf on 31/01/20.

DfE (2015) *Early Years Foundation Stage Profile Results: Additional Tables. Technical Document.* London: DfE. Retrieved from https://assets.publishing.service.gov.uk/government/uploads/system/uploads/attachment_data/file/477872/SFR36_2015_Technical_Document_Additional_Tables.pdf on 26/02/20.

DfE (2016) 'Government school workforce survey.' Retrieved from https://assets.publishing.service.gov.uk/government/uploads/system/uploads/attachment_data/file/620825/SFR25_2017_MainText.pdf on 26/02/20.

DfE (2017) *Early Years Foundation Stage Profile Results in England.* London: DfE. Retrieved from https://assets.publishing.service.gov.uk/government/uploads/system/uploads/attachment_data/file/652602/SFR60_2017_Text.pdf on 05/02/20.

DfE (2018) *Schools, Pupils and Their Characteristics: January 2018*. London: DfE. Retrieved from https://assets.publishing.service.gov.uk/government/ uploads/system/uploads/attachment_data/file/719226/Schools_Pupils_ and_their_Characteristics_2018_Main_Text.pdf on 05/02/20.

DfE (2019) *Schools, Pupils and Their Characteristics, 2019*. London: DfE. Retrieved from https://assets.publishing.service.gov.uk/ government/uploads/system/uploads/attachment_data/file/812539/ Schools_Pupils_and_their_Characteristics_2019_Main_Text.pdf?_ ga=2.172957091.1674443009.1566565777-393041023.1531154718 on 05/02/20.

Dixon, K. (2018) 'Seven reasons for teachers to welcome home languages in education.' Retrieved from www.britishcouncil.org/voices-magazine/ reasons-for-teachers-to-prioritise-home-languages-in-education on 31/01/20.

Dunham, Y., Baron, A.S. and Banaji, M.R. (2008) 'The development of implicit intergroup cognition.' *Trends in Cognitive Sciences 12*, 248–253.

Earick, M. (2008) *Racially Equitable Teaching: Beyond the Whiteness of Professional Development for Early Childhood Teachers*. New York: Peter Lang.

Eaude, T. (2018) 'Fundamental British values? Possible implications for children's spirituality.' *International Journal of Children's Spirituality 23*, 1, 67–80.

El Sharif, J. (2010) 'Understanding parents' perspectives on inclusive education and partnership practice: A life history approach.' Unpublished PhD thesis, University of Birmingham.

Equality Act (2010) c.15. Retrieved from www.legislation.gov.uk/ ukpga/2010/15/pdfs/ukpga_20100015_en.pdf on 02/02/20.

Eurostat (2018) 'Your key to European statistics.' Retrieved from https:// ec.europa.eu/eurostat/web/products-eurostat-news/-/EDN-20180926-1 on 02/04/20.

Evans, G. (2016) *Educational Failure and Working Class White Children in Britain*. Basingstoke: Palgrave Macmillan.

Evans, M., Schneider, C., Arnot, M., Fisher, L., Forbes, K., Hu, M. and Liu, Y. (2016) *Language Development and School Achievement: Opportunities and Challenges in the Education of EAL Students*. Cambridge: Bell Foundation.

Farrell, P. (2004) 'School psychologists making inclusion a reality for all.' *School Psychology International 25*, 5–19.

Fazel, M. (2015) 'A moment of change: Facilitating refugee children's mental health in UK schools.' *International Journal of Educational Development 41*, 255–261.

Flood, A. (2018) 'Ethnic diversity in UK children's books to be examined.' Retrieved from www.theguardian.com/books/2018/feb/07/ethnic-diversity-uk-childrens-books-arts-council-england-representation on 02/02/20.

Foley, Y., Anderson, C., Conteh, J. and Hancock, J. (2018) *Initial Teacher Education and English as an Additional Language: Research Report*. Edinburgh: The Bell Foundation and Unbound Philanthropy. Retrieved from www.ceres.education.ed.ac.uk/wp-content/uploads/ITE-Report.pdf on 02/02/20.

Ford, R. (2019) 'Up to 75% of babies are born to migrant mothers in parts of UK.' Retrieved from www.thetimes.co.uk/article/up-to-75-of-babies-are-born-to-migrant-mothers-in-parts-of-uk-j2xv9r858 on 02/02/20.

Foster Jr, H.W. (1997) 'The enigma of low birth weight and race.' *New England Journal of Medicine 337*, 17, 1232–1233.

Foster, M. (1990) 'The politics of race: Through the eyes of African-American teachers.' *Journal of Education 172*, 3, 123–141.

Gale, P. (2000) 'Construction of Whiteness in the Australian Media.' In J. Docker and G. Fischer (eds) *Race, Colour and Identity in Australia and New Zealand*. Sydney: University of New South Wales Press.

Garrett, M.T. (1998) *Walking on the Wind: Cherokee Teachings for Harmony and Balance*. Santa Fe, NM: Bear & Company.

Gay, G. and Kirkland, K. (2003) 'Developing cultural critical consciousness and self-reflection in preservice teacher education.' *Theory into Practice 42*, 3, 181–187.

Gill, D. (2013) 'Practitioners' and parents' perceptions and attitudes about bilingual education.' *Race Equality Teaching 31*, 3, 19–24.

Glyn, I.A. (n.d.) 'Heart of the nation.' Retrieved from www.wales.com/about/language/heart-nation on 02/02/20.

Goff, P.A., Jackson, M.C., Di Leone, B.A.L., Culotta, C.M. and DiTomasso, N.A. (2014) 'The essence of innocence: Consequences of dehumanizing Black children.' *Journal of Personality and Social Psychology 106*, 4, 526.

Goodman, M.E. (1964) *Race Awareness in Young Children*, 2nd edition. New York: Collier Books.

Grant, C.A. and Ladson-Billings, G. (1997) *Dictionary of Multicultural Education*. Phoenix, AZ: The Oryx Press.

Grierson, J. (2019) '"My son was terrified": How Prevent alienates UK Muslims.' *The Guardian*, 27 January. Retrieved from www.theguardian.com/uk-news/2019/jan/27/prevent-muslim-community-discrimination on 26/02/20.

Groulx, J.G. and Silva, C. (2010) 'Evaluating the development of culturally relevant teaching.' *Multicultural Perspectives 12*, 1, 3–9.

Haavind, H., Thorne, B., Hollway, W. and Magnusson, E. (2015) '"Because nobody likes Chinese girls": Intersecting identities and emotional experiences of subordination and resistance in school life.' *Childhood 22*, 3, 300–315.

Hackett, C. and Mcclenden, D. (2017) 'Christians remain world's largest religious group, but they are declining in Europe.' Retrieved from www.pewresearch.org/fact-tank/2017/04/05/christians-remain-worlds-largest-religious-group-but-they-are-declining-in-europe on 02/02/20.

Hall, E.T. (1976) *Beyond Culture*. Garden City, NY: Anchor Press.

Hamilton, P. (2013) 'Including migrant worker children in the learning and social context of the rural primary school.' *Education 3–13*, *41*, 2, 202–217.

Hazard, A.Q. (2011) 'A racialized deconstruction? Ashley Montagu and the 1950 UNESCO statement on race.' *Transforming Anthropology 19*, 2, 174–186.

Hemming, P., Hailwood, E. and Stokes, C. (2018) *Diversity of Religion and Belief: A Guidance and Resource Pack for Primary Schools in England and Wales*. Cardiff: Cardiff University.

Henry, L. ( 2016) 'The early years has more to do to embrace diversity.' Retrieved from www.nurseryworld.co.uk/nursery-world/opinion/1156673/the-early-years-has-more-to-do-to-embrace-diversity on 02/02/20.

Heron-Delaney, M., Anzures, G., Herbert, J.S., Quinn, P.C. *et al.* (2011) 'Perceptual training prevents the emergence of the other race effect during infancy.' *PloS One 6*, 5, e19858.

Hessels, M.G.P. (1997) 'Low IQ but high learning potential: Why Zeyneb and Moussa do not belong in special education.' *Educational and Child Psychology 14*, 4, 121–136.

Hick, P. (2007) 'Still Missing Out: Minority Ethnic Communities and Special Education Needs.' In B. Richardson (ed.) *Tell It Like It Is: How Our Schools Fail Black Children*, 2nd edition. London: Trentham Books.

Hill-Collins, P. (2000) 'Gender, black feminism, and black political economy.' *Annals of the American Academy of Political and Social Science 568*, 1, 41–53.

Hilliard, A.G. (2006) 'Aliens in the education matrix: Recovering freedom.' *The New Educator 2*, 87–102.

Hinman, L.M. (2003) *Ethics: A Pluralist Approach to Moral Theory*, 3rd edition. Belmont, CA: Wadsworth.

Hirschfeld, L.A. (2008) 'Children's Developing Conceptions of Race.' In S.M. Quintana and C. McKown (eds) *Handbook of Race, Racism, and the Developing Child*. New Jersey: John Wiley and Sons.

Hirschman, C. (2004) 'The origins and demise of the concept of race.' *Population and Development Review 30*, 3, 385–415.

HM Government (2010) 'Equality Act 2010 Explanatory Notes.' Retrieved from www.legislation.gov.uk/ukpga/2010/15/notes/division/3/2/1/7?view=plain on 26/02/20.

HM Government (2011) 'Prevent Strategy.' Retrieved from https://assets.publishing.service.gov.uk/government/uploads/system/uploads/attachment_data/file/97976/prevent-strategy-review.pdf on 26/02/20.

Hodal, K. (2016) 'Nearly half of all refugees are children, says Unicef.' Retrieved from www.theguardian.com/global-development/2016/sep/07/nearly-half-of-all-refugees-are-children-unicef-report-migrants-united-nations on 02/02/20.

Hoeffel, E.M., Rastogi, K., Myoung, K.O. and Hasan, S. (2012) 'Asian population: 2010.' Retrieved from www.census.gov/content/dam/Census/library/publications/2012/dec/c2010br-11.pdf on 02/02/20.

Holt, J.D. (2015) *Religious Education in the Secondary School: An Introduction to Teaching, Learning and the World Religions*. London: Taylor & Francis.

HRCR (1983) Mandla and another v Dowell Lee and another. House of Lords on 11/09/2017. Retrieved from www.hrcr.org/safrica/equality/Mandla_DowellLee.htm on 02/02/20.

Hu, J., Torr, J. and Whiteman, P. (2014) 'Australian Chinese parents' language attitudes and practices relating to their children's bilingual development prior to school.' *Journal of Early Childhood Research 12*, 2, 139–153.

Hutchinson, J. (2018) *Educational Outcomes of Children with an Additional Language*. London: Education Policy Institute.

Huyck, D. and Park S.D. (2019) 'Diversity in children's books 2018.' Retrieved from https://readingspark.wordpress.com/2019/06/19/picture-this-diversity-in-childrens-books-2018-infographic on 02/02/20.

Huyck, D., Park Dahlen, S. and Griffin, M.B. (2016) 'Diversity in children's books 2015 infographic.' Retrieved from https://readingspark.wordpress.com/2016/09/14/picture-this-reflecting-diversity-in-childrens-book-publishing on 26/02/20.

Ipgrave, J. (2010) 'Including the religious viewpoints and experiences of Muslim students in an environment that is both plural and secular.' In The Education of Minority Muslim Students Comparative Perspectives (special issue), *Journal of International Migration and Integration*, SpringerLink, 5–22.

Ipgrave, J. (2011) 'Religious diversity: Models of inclusion for schools in England.' *Canadian and International Education/Education canadienne et internationale 40*, 2, Article 7. Retrieved from http://ir.lib.uwo.ca/cie-eci/vol40/iss2/7 on 22/06/20.

Ipgrave, J. (2015) 'Interfaith Dialogue in the Classroom.' In S. Elton-Chalcraft (ed.) *Teaching Religious Education Creatively*. Abingdon: Routledge.

Jackson, R. (2004) *Rethinking Religious Education and Plurality*. London: Routledge.

Jackson, R. (2009) 'Understanding the religions and worldviews of others.' Alliance of Civilizations Forum, Istanbul, Turkey, 6 April. Retrieved from http://erb.unaoc.org/understanding-the-religions-and-worldviews-of-others on 26/02/20.

Jackson, R. and Everington, J. (2017) 'Teaching inclusive religious education impartially: An English perspective.' *British Journal of Religious Education 39*, 1, 7–24.

Jones, C. (2016) 'Taking Wales Forward: 2016–2021.' Retrieved from https://gov.wales/sites/default/files/publications/2017-08/taking-wales-forward.pdf on 26/02/20.

Jones, K. (2017) 'Developing and promoting bilingualism in Wales.' Retrieved from https://lovetoteach87.com/2016/07/24/developing-and-promoting-bilingualism-in-wales on 26/02/20.

Kalyanpur, M. (1998) 'The challenge of cultural blindness: Implications for family-focused service delivery.' *Journal of Child and Family Studies 7*, 3, 317–332.

Kaplan, J.M. (2011) '"Race": What Biology Can Tell Us about a Social Construct.' In *Encyclopedia of Life Sciences* (ELS). Chichester: John Wiley & Sons, Ltd.

Katz, P.A. and Kofkin, J.A. (1997) 'Race, Gender, and Young Children.' In S.S. Luthar, J.A. Burack, D. Cicchetti and J.R. Weisz (eds) *Developmental Psychopathology: Perspectives on Adjustment, Risk, and Disorder*. New York: Cambridge University Press.

Keddie, A. (2014) 'The politics of Britishness: Multiculturism, schooling and social cohesion.' *British Educational Research Journal 40*, 3, 539–554.

Kelly, D.J., Quinn, P.C., Slater, A.M., Lee, K. *et al.* (2005) 'Three-month-olds, but not newborns, prefer own-race faces.' *Developmental Science 8*, 6, F31–F36.

Kelly, D.J., Quinn, P.C., Slater, A.M., Lee, K., Ge, L. and Pascalis, O. (2007) 'The other-race effect develops during infancy: Evidence of perceptual narrowing.' *Psychological Science 18*, 12, 1084–1089.

Khan, K. (2009) *Preventing Violent Extremism (PVE) and PREVENT: A Response from the Muslim Community*. London: An-Nisa Society.

Kinzler, K.D. (2016) 'How kids learn prejudice.' *New York Times*, 23 October. Retrieved from www.nytimes.com/2016/10/23/opinion/sunday/how-kids-learn-prejudice.html on 26/02/20.

Klug, B.J. and Whitfield, P.T. (2003) *Widening the Circle – Culturally Relevant Pedagogy for American Indian Children*. London: Routledge.

Klode, G. (1988) 'Language Contact and Bilingualism in Switzerland.' In C.B. Paulston (ed.) *International Handbook of Bilingualism and Bilingual Education*. Westport, CT: Greenwood Press.

Knowles, G. (2011) *Supporting Inclusive Practice*, 2nd edition. Abingdon: Routledge.

Konstantoni, K. and Emejulu, A. (2017) 'When intersectionality met childhood studies: The dilemmas of a travelling concept.' *Children's Geographies 15*, 1, 6–22.

Krashen, S. (1987) *Principles and Practice in Second Language Acquisition*. Hemel Hempstead: Prentice-Hall International.

Kroeber, A.L. and Kluckhohn, C. (1952) 'Culture: A critical review of concepts and definitions.' *Harvard University Peabody Museum of American Archeology and Ethnology Papers 4*.

Kustatscher, M. (2017) 'The emotional geographies of belonging: Children's intersectional identities in primary school.' *Children's Geographies 15*, 1, 65–79.

Ladson-Billings, G. (1994) *The Dreamkeepers*. San Francisco, CA: Jossey-Bass Publishing Co.

Ladson-Billings, G. (1995) 'Toward a theory of culturally relevant pedagogy.' *American Educational Research Journal 32*, 465–491.

Lambert, W.E. (1983) 'Deciding on Languages of Instruction: Psychological and Social Considerations.' In T. Husen and S. Opper (eds) *Multicultural and Multilingual Education in Immigrant Countries*. Oxford: Pergamon Press.

la Rivière Zijdel, L. (2009) 'The Ignored Aspects of Intersectionality.' In B.M. Bagilhole, Cabó, A., Franken, M. and Woodward, A. (eds) *Teaching Intersectionality – Putting Gender at the Centre*. Published by ATHENA3 Advanced Thematic Network in Women's Studies in Europe, University of Utrecht and Centre for Gender Studies, Stockholm University.

Lauchlan, F. and Boyle, C. (2007) 'Is the use of labels in special education helpful?' *Support for Learning 22*, 1, 36–42.

Lee, K., Quinn, P.C. and Pascalis, O. (2017) 'Face race processing and racial bias in early development: A perceptual-social linkage.' *Current Directions in Psychological Science 26*, 3, 256–262.

Lee, S. (2019) 'Race, power, and minority parent participation.' *Phi Delta Kappan 101*, 1, 30–33.

Leonardo, Z. (2002) 'The souls of white folk: Critical pedagogy, whiteness studies, and globalization discourse.' *Race Ethnicity & Education 5*, 1, 29–50.

Levy, S.R., West, T.L., Ramirez, L.F. and Pachankis, J.E. (2004) 'Racial and ethnic prejudice among children.' *The Psychology of Prejudice and Discrimination: Racism in America 1*, 37–60.

Lijphart, A. (1981) *Conflict and Coexistence in Belgium: The Dynamics of a Culturally Divided Society* (No. 46). Berkeley, CA: University of California Press.

Linton, R. (1945) *The Cultural Background of Personality*. New York: Appleton-Century.

Lloyd, E. (2018) 'Underpaid and undervalued: The reality of childcare work in the UK.' Retrieved from https://theconversation.com/underpaid-and-undervalued-the-reality-of-childcare-work-in-the-uk-87413 on 26/02/20.

Lloyd, T. (2011) 'Boys' underachievement in schools: Literature review.' Retrieved from www.boysdevelopmentproject.org.uk/wp-content/uploads/2013/06/Boys-and-underachievement-literature-review-edited-in-pdf.pdf on 26/02/20.

Lockley-Scott, A. (2019) 'Towards a critique of fundamental British values: The case of the classroom.' *Journal of Beliefs & Values 40*, 3, 354–367.

Loewen, S. (2004) 'Second Language Concerns for Refugee Children.' In R. Hamilton and D. Moore (eds) *Educational Interventions for Refugee Children*. London: Routledge Falmer.

Luft, J., Ingham, H. (1955) 'The Johari window, a graphic model of interpersonal awareness.' *Proceedings of the Western Training Laboratory in Group Development*. Los Angeles: University of California, Los Angeles.

Lykke, N. (2010) *Feminist Studies: A Guide to Intersectional Theory, Methodology and Writing*. New York: Routledge.

Lynch, E. and Hanson, M. (1998) *Developing Cross-Cultural Competence*. Baltimore, MD: Paul H Brookes.

MacNaughton, G. (2009) 'Equity Issues in Early Childhood Teacher Learning in Australia.' In *Beyond Pedagogies of Exclusion in Diverse Childhood Contexts*. New York: Palgrave Macmillan.

MacNaughton, G. and Davis, K. (eds) (2009) *Race and Early Childhood Education: An International Approach to Identity, Politics, and Pedagogy*. New York: Springer.

Manzoni, C. and Rolfe, H. (2019) 'How schools are integrating new migrant pupils and their families.' Retrieved from www.niesr.ac.uk/sites/default/files/publications/MigrantChildrenIntegrationFinalReport.pdf on 26/02/20.

Marfelt, M.M. (2016) 'Grounded intersectionality: Key tensions, a methodological framework, and implications for diversity research.' *Equality, Diversity and Inclusion: An International Journal 35*, 1, 31–47.

Martin, J. and McCracken, M. (2018) 'Finding young EAL learners' voices: Using Google Translate in class.' *EAL Journal*, 21 May. Retrieved from https://ealjournal.org/2018/05/21/finding-young-eal-learners-voices-using-google-translate-in-class on 03/02/20.

Maylor, U. (2010) 'Notions of diversity, British identities and citizenship belonging.' *Race Ethnicity and Education 13*, 2, 233–252.

Maylor, U. (2016) '"I'd worry about how to teach it": British values in English classrooms.' *Journal of Education for Teaching 42*, 3, 314–328.

McKirdy, E. (2016) 'Nearly 50 million children are refugees or migrants.' Retrieved from www.cnn.com/2016/09/07/world/unicef-report-on-child-refugees-and-migrants/index.html on 03/02/20.

Meece, D. and Wingate, K.O.K. (2010) 'Providing early childhood teachers with opportunities to understand diversity and the achievement gap.' *SRATE Journal 19*, 1, 36–43.

Morning, A. (2015) 'Ethnic classification in global perspective: A cross-national survey of the 2000 census round.' In Simon, P., Piché, V. and Gagnon, A.A. (eds) *Social Statistics and Ethnic Diversity*. Springer, Cham (pp.17–37).

Moss, P. (2006) 'Structures, understandings and discourses: Possibilities for re-envisioning the early childhood worker.' *Contemporary Issues in Early Childhood 7*, 1, 30–41.

Moulin-Stożek, D. and Metcalfe, J. (2018) 'Mapping the moral assumptions of multi-faith religious education.' *British Journal of Religious Education*, 1–10.

NAEYC (n.d.) 'What is anti-bias education?' Retrieved from www.naeyc.org/sites/default/files/globally-shared/downloads/PDFs/resources/topics/Chap1_Anti-Bias%20Education.pdf on 03/02/20.

NALDIC (2019) 'NALDIC's response to Ofsted's draft education inspection framework for 2019.' Retrieved from https://ealjournal.org/2019/04/03/naldics-response-to-ofsteds-draft-education-inspection-framework-for-2019 on 26/02/20.

NAME (2020) 'Definitions of multicultural education.' Retrieved from www.nameorg.org/definitions_of_multicultural_e.php on 26/02/20.

Nargis, R. and Tikly, T. (2010) *Guidelines for Inclusion and Diversity in Schools*. Madrid: British Council.

National Assembly for Wales (2010) 'The Teaching and Acquisition of Welsh as a Second Language. September 2010.' Retrieved from https://senedd.wales/NAfW%20Documents/the_teaching_and_acquisition_of_welsh_as_a_second_language_-_e.pdf%20-%2028092010/the_teaching_and_acquisition_of_welsh_as_a_second_language_-_e-English.pdf on 22/06/20.

National Secular Society (2019) 'Britain's non-religious population growing rapidly, figures show.' Retrieved from www.secularism.org.uk/news/2019/04/britains-non-religious-population-growing-rapidly-figures-show on 26/02/20.

NATRE (2019) 'What are Ofsted inspectors saying about Religious Education? – the first 101 reports that mention RE.' Retrieved from www.natre.org. uk/uploads/Ofsted%20Primary%20and%20Secondary%20Reports%20 Autumn%202019%20221119%20final%20final.pdf on 26/02/20.

NCTL (2015) 'Newly Qualified Teachers: Annual Survey 2015.' Retrieved from www.gov.uk/government/uploads/system/uploads/attachment_data/ file/477461/Newly_Qualified_Teachers_Annual_Survey_2015.pdf on 03/02/20.

O'Connor, K. and Zeichner, K. (2011) 'Preparing US teachers for critical global education.' *Globalisation, Societies and Education 9*, 3–4, 521–536.

OECD (2017) 'Teachers in diverse societies.' Proceedings of the Second Policy Forum. Retrieved from www.oecd.org/education/school/Forum-Proceedings-final.pdf on 03/02/20.

Ofsted (2014) 'Overcoming barriers: Ensuring that Roma children are fully engaged and achieving in education.' Retrieved from https:// assets.publishing.service.gov.uk/government/uploads/system/uploads/ attachment_data/file/430866/Overcoming_barriers_-_ensuring_that_ Roma_children_are_fully_engaged_and_achieving_in_education.pdf on 03/02/20.

Ofsted (2017) *School Inspection Handbook: Handbook for Inspecting Schools in England under Section 5 of the Education Act 2005.* Manchester: Ofsted. Retrieved from https://dera.ioe.ac.uk/30206/1/School_inspection_ handbook_section_5.pdf on 26/02/20.

ONS (2001) 'Census: Special Migration Statistics (United Kingdom). UK Data Service Census Support.' Retreived from https://wicid.ukdataservice.ac.uk on 22/06/20.

ONS (2011a) 'Census analysis: Ethnicity and religion of the non UK born population in England and Wales.' Retrieved from www.ons. gov.uk/peoplepopulationandcommunity/ culturalidentity/ethnicity/ articles/2011censusanalysisethnicity andreligionofthenonukborn populationinenglandandwales/2015-06-18 on 03/02/20.

ONS (2011b) '2011 Census analysis: What does the 2011 Census tell us about inter-ethnic relationships?' Retrieved from www.ons.gov. uk/peoplepopulationandcommunity/birthsdeathsandmarriages/ marriagecohabitationandcivilpartnerships/articles/whatdoesthe2011 censustellusaboutinterethnicrelationships/2014-07-03 on 03/02/20.

ONS (2011c) '2011 Census analysis: What does the 2011 Census tell us about the characteristics of Gypsy or Irish Travellers in England and Wales?' Retrieved from www.ons.gov.uk/peoplepopulationandcommunity/culturalidentity/ ethnicity/articles/whatdoesthe2011censustellusaboutthecharacteristics ofgypsyoririshtravellersinenglandandwales/2014-01-21 on 26/02/20.

ONS (2013) 'Full story: What does the Census tell us about religion in 2011? Retrieved from https://www.ons.gov.uk/peoplepopulationandcommunity/culturalidentity/religion/articles/fullstorywhatdoesthecensustellusaboutreligionin2011/2013-05-16#:~:text=In%20the%202011%20Census%2C%20Christians,of%20the%20main%20religious%20groups.&text=People%20with%20no%20religion%20had%20a%20younger%20age%20profile%20than,cent)%20were%20aged%20under%2050 on 22/06/20.

Page, J. and Whitting, G. (2007) 'Engaging Effectively with Black and Minority Ethnic Parents in Children's and Parental Services.' Research report no DCSF RR013, DCSF. Retrieved from https://dera.ioe.ac.uk/6735/2/DCSF-RR013.pdf on 03/02/20.

Pagett, L. (2006) 'Mum and Dad prefer me to speak Bengali at home: Code switching and parallel speech in a primary school setting.' *Literacy 40*, 3, 137–145.

Paine, L. (1990) *Orientation towards Diversity: What do Prospective Teachers Bring?* (Vol. 89, No. 9). National Center for Research on Teacher Education, Michigan State University.

Paris, D. (2012) 'Culturally sustaining pedagogy: A needed change in stance, terminology, and practice.' *Educational Researcher 41*, 3, 93–97.

Philips, T. (2015) 'Is it time to ditch the term "black, Asian and minority ethnic" (BAME)?' Retrieved from www.theguardian.com/commentisfree/2015/may/22/black-asian-minority-ethnic-bame-bme-trevor-phillips-racial-minorities on 03/02/20.

Phoenix, A. (2010) 'Ethnicities.' In M. Wetherell and C.T. Mohanty (eds) *Sage Handbook of Identities*. Los Angeles, CA: Sage Publications.

Picchio, M. and Mayer, S. (2019) 'Transitions in ECEC services: The experience of children from migrant families.' *European Early Childhood Education Research Journal 27*, 2, 285–296.

Pizzillo, J.J. (1983) *Intercultural Studies*. Dubuque, IA: Kendall/Hunt.

Porfilio, B.J. and Malott, C.S. (2011) 'Guiding White pre-service and in-service teachers toward critical pedagogy: Utilizing counter-cultures in teacher education.' *Educational Foundations 25*, 63–81.

Priest, N., Walton, J., White, F., Kowal, E., Fox, B. and Paradies, Y. (2016) 'You are not born being racist, are you? Discussing racism with primary-aged children.' *Race Ethnicity and Education 19*, 4, 808–834.

Ramdarshan Bold, M. (2019) *Representation of People of Colour among Children's Book Authors and Illustrators*. BookTrust Represents, UK.

Ramsey, P.G. (1982) 'Multicultural education in early childhood.' *Young Children 37*, 2, 13–24.

REC (2018) 'Chronic shortage of RE teachers in schools.' Retrieved from www.religiouseducationcouncil.org.uk/news/chronic-shortage-re-teachers-schools on 26/02/20.

Sak, R., Rohrmann, T., Şahin Sak, İ.T. and Schauer, G. (2019) 'Parents' views on male ECEC workers: A cross-country comparison.' *European Early Childhood Education Research Journal 27*, 1, 68–80.

Save the Children (2016) 'World refugee crisis explained: The worst refugees crisis since WWII.' Retrieved from www.savethechildren.org/us/what-we-do/emergency-response/refugee-children-crisis on 03/02/20.

Sellgreen, K. (2018) 'Lack of good religious education "leaves pupils at risk".' 16 February. Retrieved from www.bbc.co.uk/news/education-43073161 on 03/02/20.

Sherwood, H. (2017) 'More than half UK population has no religion.' Retrieved from www.theguardian.com/world/2017/sep/04/half-uk-population-has-no-religion-british-social-attitudes-survey on 03/02/20.

Sherwood, H. (2019) 'UK secularism on rise as more than half say they have no religion.' Retrieved from www.theguardian.com/world/2019/jul/11/uk-secularism-on-rise-as-more-than-half-say-they-have-no-religion on 03/02/20.

Sikan, S. (2007) 'Multilingual children in monolingual centres.' *Children in Europe 12*, 15–17.

Simpson, L., Jivraj, S. and Warren, J. (2016) 'The stability of ethnic identity in England and Wales 2001–2011.' *Journal of the Royal Statistical Society: Series A (Statistics in Society) 179*, 4, 1025–1049.

Siraj-Blatchford, I. (1994) *The Early Years: Laying the Foundations for Racial Equality*. Stoke-on-Trent: Trentham Books Limited.

Siraj-Blatchford, I. and Clarke, P. (2000) *Supporting Identity, Diversity and Language in the Early Years*. London: McGraw-Hill Education (UK).

Standards and Testing Agency (2017) 'Early Years Foundation Stage Profile 2018 Handbook.' Retrieved from https://assets.publishing.service.gov.uk/government/uploads/system/uploads/attachment_data/file/669079/Early_years_foundation_stage_profile_2018_handbook.pdf on 26/02/20.

Standards and Testing Agency (2018) 'Early Years Foundation Stage Profile 2019 Handbook.' Retrieved from https://assets.publishing.service.gov.uk/government/uploads/system/uploads/attachment_data/file/790580/EYFSP_Handbook_2019.pdf on 02/04/20.

Stern, J. (2018) *Teaching Religious Education: Researchers in the Classroom* 2nd edition. London: Bloomsbury Publishing.

Strand, S. (2007) *Minority Ethnic Pupils in the Longitudinal Study of Young People in England*. DCSF Research Report RR-002. London: DCSF. Retrieved from www.dfes.gov.uk/research/data/uploadfiles/DCSF-RR002.pdf on 26/02/20.

Strand, S. and Demie, F. (2006) 'Pupil mobility, attainment and progress in primary school.' *British Educational Research Journal 32*, 4, 551–568.

Strangeways-Booth, A. (2017) 'Schools break law on religious education, research suggests.' Retrieved from www.bbc.co.uk/news/education-41282330 on 03/02/20.

Suárez-Orozco, M. (2001) 'Globalization, immigration, and education: The research agenda.' *Harvard Educational Review 71*, 3, 345–366.

Sue, D.W., Capodilupo, C.M., Torino, G.C., Bucceri, J.M., Holder, A., Nadal, K.L. and Esquilin, M. (2007) 'Racial microaggressions in everyday life: Implications for clinical practice.' *American Psychologist 62*, 4, 271.

Sunak, R. and Rajeswaran, S. (2014) *A Portrait of Modern Britain*. London: Policy Exchange.

Syal, R. (2017) 'More than 600,000 pupils in England taught by unqualified teachers.' *The Guardian*, 25 July. Retrieved from www.theguardian.com/education/2017/jul/25/more-than-600000-pupils-in-england-taught-by-unqualified-teachers on 03/02/20.

Taylor, F. (2013) 'Multilingual Britain.' Retrieved from www.thebritishacademy.ac.uk/sites/default/files/Multilingual%20Britain%20Report.pdf on 03/02/20.

Tiedt, P. and Tiedt, I.M. (1990) *Multicultural Teaching: A Handbook of Activities, Information, and Resources*. Boston, MA: Allyn and Bacon.

Turner, C. (2017) 'Catholic school prompts uniform row by banning Muslim girl from wearing a headscarf.' *The Telegraph*, 23 January. Retrieved from www.telegraph.co.uk/education/2017/01/23/catholic-school-prompts-uniform-row-banning-muslim-girl-wearing on 03/02/20.

Turner, R. (2017) 'Muslim parents sending their children to Christian schools to prepare them for "life in modern Britain"', *The Telegraph*, 20 February. Retrieved from https://www.telegraph.co.uk/education/2017/02/20/muslim-parents-send-children-christian-schools-toprepare-life on 22/06/20.

Ukpokodu, O.N. (2004) 'The impact of shadowing culturally different students on preservice teachers' disposition toward diversity.' *Multicultural Education 12*, 2, 19–28.

UNESCO (1950a) 'The Race question.' Retrieved from https://unesdoc.unesco.org/ark:/48223/pf0000128291 on 26/02/20.

UNESCO (1950b) 'Fallacies of racism exposed: UNESCO publishes declaration by world's scientists.' *UNESCO Courier 3*, 6/7, 1–16. Retrieved from https://en.unesco.org/courier/july-august-1950 on 26/02/20.

UNESCO (2005) 'Guidelines for inclusion: Ensuring access to education for all.' Retrieved from https://unesdoc.unesco.org/ark:/48223/pf0000140224 on 03/02/20.

UNICEF (1989) 'Fact sheet: A summary of the rights under the Convention on the Rights of the Child.' Retrieved from www.unicef.org/crc/files/Rights_overview.pdf on 03/02/20.

University of Manchester (2013) 'Geographies of diversity in Manchester.' Retrieved from http://hummedia.manchester.ac.uk/institutes/code/briefings/localdynamicsofdiversity/geographies-of-diversity-in-manchester.pdf on 03/02/20.

Van Ausdale, D. and Feagin, J.R. (2001) *The First R: How Children Learn Race and Racism*. Lanham, MD: Rowman & Littlefield Publishers.

Van Hook, C.W. (2002) 'Preservice teachers' perceived barriers to the implementation of a multicultural curriculum.' *Journal of Instructional Psychology 29*, 4, 254–265.

van Krieken Robson, J. (2019) 'How do practitioners in early years provision promote Fundamental British Values?' *International Journal of Early Years Education 27*, 1, 95–110.

Van Laere, K. and Vandenbroeck, M. (2017) 'Early learning in preschool: Meaningful and inclusive for all? Exploring perspectives of migrant parents and staff.' *European Early Childhood Education Research Journal* 25, 2, 243–257.

Vandenbroeck, M. (2008) 'Positive Identities in a Changing World.' In L. Brooker and M. Woodhead (eds) *Developing Positive Identities. Early Childhood in Focus, 3.* Milton Keynes: Child and Youth Studies Group, Open University.

Vandenbroeck, M. (2011) 'Diversity in Early Childhood Services.' In J. Bennett (ed.) *Encyclopedia on Early Childhood Development.* Montreal: Centre of Excellence for Early Childhood Development and Strategic Knowledge Cluster on Early Child Development.

Vega, T. (2017) 'Where are you "really" from? Try another question.' Retrieved from www.cnn.com/2017/06/20/opinions/where-are-you-really-from-vega-opinion/index.html on 03/02/20.

Versi, M. (2017) 'The latest Prevent figures show why the strategy needs an independent review.' *The Guardian,* 10 November. Retrieved from www.theguardian.com/commentisfree/2017/nov/10/prevent-strategy-statistics-independent-review-home-office-muslims on 03/02/20.

Wales Education (2017) 'Education in Wales: Our national mission. Action plan 2017–2021.' Retrieved from https://gov.wales/sites/default/files/publications/2018-02/welsh-in-education-action-plan-2017%E2%80%9321.pdf on 03/02/20.

Wardle, F. and Cruz-Janzen, M. (2004) *Meeting the Needs of Multiethnic and Multiracial Children in Schools.* Boston, MA: Allyn & Bacon.

Warin, J. (2018) 'Fathers and Male Preschool Workers.' In *Men in Early Childhood Education and Care. Palgrave Studies in Gender and Education.* London: Palgrave Macmillan.

Warin, J. (2019) 'Conceptualising the value of male practitioners in early childhood education and care: Gender balance or gender flexibility.' *Gender and Education 31,* 3, 293–308.

Weale, A. (2019) 'Drive aims to increase number of men in early years education in UK.' *The Guardian,* 13 January. Retrieved from www.theguardian.com/education/2019/jan/13/drive-aims-increase-number-men-early-years-education on 03/02/20.

Weale, S. and Adams, R. (2016) 'Schools must focus on struggling White working-class pupils, says UK charity.' *The Guardian,* 10 November. Retrieved from www.theguardian.com/education/2016/nov/10/schools-focus-struggling-white-working-class-pupils-uk on 26/02/20.

Welsh Government (2018) 'New school curriculum: What's changing?' Retrieved from http://gov.wales/topics/educationandskills/schoolshome/curriculuminwales/curriculum-for-walescurriculum-for-life/?lang=en on 26/02/20.

Williams, A. and Steele, J.R. (2019) 'Examining children's implicit racial attitudes using exemplar and category-based measures.' *Child Development 90,* e322–e338. doi: 10.1111/cdev.12991

Wilson, T. (2015) *Hospitality and Translation: An Exploration of How Muslim Pupils Translate their Faith in the Context of an Anglican Primary School.* Newcastle: Cambridge Scholars Publishing.

Winterbottom, C. (2013) 'Voices of the minority: Japanese immigrant mothers' perceptions of preschools in the United States.' *Early Childhood Education Journal 41*, 3, 219–225.

Wong, L. (2019) '"Where are you really from?" How to navigate this question of race and identity.' Retrieved from www.abc.net.au/life/where-are-you-really-from-how-to-better-ask-race-question/10610346 on 03/02/20.

Wong, S.W. and Hughes, J.N. (2006) 'Ethnicity and language contributions to dimensions of parent involvement.' *School Psychology Review 35*, 4, 645.

Woodhead, M. and Oates, J. (2008) *Developing Positive Identities: Diversity and Young Children.* Early Childhood in Focus 3. Milton Keynes: Open University Press.

Xiaoxia, L. (1999) 'How can language minority parents help their children become bilingual in familial context? A case study of a language minority mother and her daughter.' *Bilingual Research Journal 23*, 2–3, 211–223.

Yuval-Davis, N. (2006) 'Intersectionality and feminist politics.' *European Journal of Women's Studies 13*, 3, 193–209.

Yuval-Davis, N. (2011) 'Power, intersectionality and the politics of belonging.' FREIA (Feminist Research Center in Aalborg), Aalborg University, Denmark.

Zimmerman, K.A. (2017) 'What is culture?' Retrieved from www.livescience.com/21478-what-is-culture-definition-of-culture.html on 03/02/20.

# Subject Index

Sub-headings in *italics* indicate figures.

# Author Index

la Rivière Zijdel, L. 141
Ladson-Billings, G. 49, 90–1
Lambert, W.E. 110
Lauchlan, F. 13
Lee, K. 39
Lee, S. 101
Leman, P.J. 37
Leonardo, Z. 122
Levy, S.R. 37
Lijphart, A. 108
Linton, R. 80
Lloyd, E. 158
Lloyd, T. 157
Lockley-Scott, A. 70
Loewen, S. 18
Lopez-Robertson, J. 45
Luckner, J. 44
Luft, J. 20
Lykke, N. 140
Lynch, E. 96

MacNaughton, G. 37
Malott, C.S. 96
Manzoni, C. 18
Marfelt, M.M. 139
Martin, J. 134
Mayer, S. 100
Maylor, U. 70–1
Mcclenden, D. 56
McCracken, M. 134
McGrath, S. 44
McKirdy, E. 24
McClelland, E. 86
Meece, D. 100
Merryman, A. 39
Metcalfe, J. 72
Morning, A. 28
Moss, P. 157
Moulin-Stożek, D. 72

National Association for the
    Education of Young
    Children (NAEYC) 99
NALDIC 121
National Association for
    Multicultural Education
    (NAME) 89

Nargis, R. 9
National Assembly for Wales 127
National Secular Society 55
National Association of
    Teachers of Religious
    Education (NATRE) 59
NCTL 117

O'Connor, K. 21
O'Malley, J.M. 123
Office of National Statistics
    (ONS) 23, 34, 36, 54, 55
Organisation for Economic Co-
    operation and Development
    (OECD) 18–19
Ofsted 70, 147

Page, J. 147
Paine, L. 10
Paris, D. 91
Park Dahlen, S. 47–8
Pascalis, O. 39
Philips, T. 29
Phoenix, A. 141
Picchio, M. 100
Pizzillo, J.J. 92
Porfilio, B.J. 96
Powers-Costello, E. 45
Priest, N. 24, 147, 178
Quinn, P.C. 39
Ramdarshan Bold, M. 133
Ramsey, P.G. 99
Religious Education
    Council (REC) 59
Rolfe, H. 18

Safford, P. 86
Sak, R. 158
Save the Children 23–4
Sellgreen, K. 59
Sherwood, H. 56
Sikan, S. 18
Silva, C. 91
Simpson, L. 28, 29
Siraj-Blatchford, I. 18, 81
Standards and Testing Agency 120